SURVIVING SOBRIETY

RECOVERY STORIES & POEMS

PHILIP W. NATALE, III

Contents

Dedication

This book is dedicated to my sister Lisa, who passed away last June. She is missed greatly.

Introduction

This book is a collection of stories and poems written mostly in my early recovery years from 2006 to 2010. Those years are, in fact, the first five years of my new and sober life. I first quit using drugs in early 2004, but it wasn't until 2006 that I truly started getting it right, and I would also clean up the last holdover legal problems from my addicted life. It is a stew of stories and poems reflecting the people, places and things that my environment presented to me on a daily basis. The book serves as a chronicle of my early recovery years.

A Future Near Enough to Taste

It's been deflated energy from Jump Street today. The defeats of the past 24 hours outweigh the victories.

I'm close to the finish line, and my desperate need to cross it makes me a bit crazy. I know the solution to my problems will create new problems; solutions always do. It's key to know that.

My only pair of pants, my only good shirt and my only decent pair of socks were stolen. They were all freshly washed and dried. Hand washed, wrung, and air dried, shelter style.

They were stolen from their hiding place, under the mattress of my assigned bunk of the day. My tape player, the Bill Evans tape, and my Norton reader, "Uses of The Imagination," were gone, too.

I'm lucky that I have clothes to wear, which the shelter gave me last week. Still, the pants look like the pants that all the bums wear, and I'm very self-conscious about looking the part.

I'm embarrassed and sometimes ashamed of being a man with no home of his own and no income against the storm.

I'm putting the last pieces in the puzzle of dignity: a

measure of self-esteem and a modicum crumb of comfort. But in the meantime, this shelter situation is trying, nonetheless.

I've got the unaddicted part down pat. I got my Social Security disability check reinstated. I've got a couple of leads for part-time work, which I'm allowed, and an eye on a room, which I'll be able to afford when my first check comes in.

This may not come easily; it may come with difficulty. I'll need to find a landlord who is not worried about references. That may preclude a comfortable room in a house in the suburbs and get me a shithole in the city. That's okay. It's a big step up for me, and I'll get the nicer place in due course.

Ultimately, it's a new beginning, and new beginnings don't come easy. Besides, I'll do nicely wherever I am because I'll be out of the shelter and in the privacy of my own place.

I look forward to being able to smoke a cigarette in peace and privacy. Or not. I will embrace being able to write whenever I want to write or put the lights on or off, as I wish.

I look forward to simple things, when and how I choose, such as getting laid, getting a Coke from my own refrigerator, writing a letter, talking on the phone, watching the Red Sox, reinventing rocket science, getting published.

And no more washing and wringing clothes by hand.

Country in the City

I grew up in the country, and although I've lived for decades in the city, and I'm comfortable enough in it, there's a large part of me that prefers the country and country things. Pace, sky and open vistas are not the least of those things. I suppose I'm always searching for, and finding some of those things in whatever I can in the city.

I left the apartment around 8:30 pm, in bare feet and shorts, searching for headache relief, and a break from the light claustrophobia and general unease, that I'd been feeling from being cooped up inside. It doesn't take much to feel claustrophobic and anxious with this post drug-addiction traumatic stress I've gotten myself into. I thought a little time outdoors, long enough to smoke a couple of cigarettes in the fresh evening air, might ease it.

Walkman in hand, headphones on my ears, I took my leave of the apartment. I trundled down the two flights of stairs and exited the building out into the summer twilight. Passing through the courtyard, I continued until I was off the property, and out on the city sidewalk.

It was Memorial Day, and the first hot day of the very short and sweet New England warm season. The unofficial start of summer. It had been a miserably long, rainy and cold spring, practically a double winter.

Settling down to muster up a bit more enthusiasm, I came to a halt and relaxed in front of the parking meter that's adjacent to the front walk.

The claustrophobia was already breaking when I looked up and saw it. It was the moon, low and lighting the sky, a generous silver-slivered crescent and well defined. There was a thick semi-circle of clear, bright light outlining the entire, mostly voided sphere. Earth shine or moonshine, I almost never know which it is.

Given the spillage from the artificial lights in this city, the light pollution of our sky is so bad, I often can't pick up even the most brilliant stars or much of the moon. So, I was pleasantly surprised by the bright, sharp view of tonight's moon. My evening was off to a good start.

Under the influence of its portion of the day's sun, the cement sidewalk was still warm and became a comfortable overshoe on my bare feet.

The bricks on the outside wall of the apartment building were reassuringly warm, too, and provided a measure of satisfaction that my primary mission for coming outside had been well chosen for relieving my claustrophobia and anxiety, and the headache as well.

This warm evening, on top of the first hot day of the year, goes a long way towards wringing the long, hard winter from my bones.

Next

The next cigarette to smoke, the next meal to eat,
next book to read,
next relationship,
next marriage,
the next life.

The next sunny day,
the next inspiration,
next winning bet,
next family squabble,
the next paycheck.

The next hurdle,
the next murder,
next rainstorm,
next crying baby,
next phone call,
the next Sunday morning.

The next smile from Heaven.
The next dish to wash,
the next song to sing,
next neighbor to greet,
next weather report,
next buck to pass,
the next milestone to eclipse.

The next beautiful girl,
the next mistaken identity,
next spring bloom,
next person in line,
next funeral,
the next time.

The next second wind,
the next third time's a charm,
next last-ditch attempt,
next old times sake.

The next cloud across the moon,
the next moon across the sky,
next dream in my sleep,
next night that brings my rest.

Photo of a Building

Posted by the Boston Globe's Matt Rocheleau to the digital Boston Globe on November 29, 2010, 4:03 pm.

"Photo of a Building" was presented as the feature, "First Person: Giving Thanks for a Shelter from the Storm."

Newton native Philip Natale, III, 56, credits two Boston homeless shelters for helping rescue him from homelessness and drug addiction, and he offers a story of hope for those facing similar situations.

The small photo of a building on the Roxbury/South End line in the paper, with the caption, "Residents face an identity crisis," jumped out at me like gangbusters. I recognized it immediately, even though the ground floor isn't in the photo, and there's no description of what it is. It is the Woods-Mullen Shelter on Mass. Ave., a place I went to daily from 2000-2003 and continued to attend until July 2006, when I was homeless.

Funny that from my home in Palm Beach, Florida, that building would jump out at me and bring back a ton of memories from my life when I was fighting major adversity.

I have nothing but good feelings about it and the people from the Boston Health Dept. who work there, providing sanity and safety to those of us who, for various reasons, needed the help. I am also grateful that I got out; homeless life is difficult and too often ensnares people permanently.

I was dealing with a head injury, drug addiction, and poverty, and I don't know what would have become of me without the support of the shelter. I've recovered from all of it and wanted to say 'thanks', and 'God bless' to the people at Woods-Mullen and its sister shelter, Long Island Shelter.

I had suffered several instances of misfortune over a rather long period of time that ultimately resulted in my being homeless beginning in 2000.

I had been in a car accident in 1981 while delivering paychecks for my boss in his van. The van had a blowout in the Copley Square tunnel, rolled over and flipped, and although I didn't have a scratch on me, I suffered a broken neck.

This led to a dual drug addiction to the medications I was on. I was able to manage the addiction for a time, but the longer it went on, the less I was in control of my life.

In 1994, I was running in the Hyannis bus depot when I ran head-first into an air conditioner that extended out from the wall where we boarded the buses. I sustained a bad concussion, and the injury to my brain resulted in repeated concussions between the years 1994-2002.

In the 1990's after I was divorced, I raised my oldest son while being a weekend dad to my other two sons. It was in 1999, when my oldest son moved out to stake his own claim in the world, that I began to experience real difficulty.

My addiction to Valium and Klonopin had been getting worse, and I could no longer manage with my monthly, legitimate prescriptions. I began buying pills off the street, going to crooked doctors and filling forged prescriptions at drug stores.

On-and-off concussions and Benzo addiction had left me depressed, and I wasn't coping well in my life, generally. Another major problem was the financial drain of buying illicit Benzos to feed my addiction. After breaking my neck in 1981, I'd been living on Social Security Disability Insurance, which didn't leave much after basic bills.

After my son moved out in 1999, I moved from my apartment into a roominghouse in Malden Square. When I'd been there a mere 4 months, it came to light that the building wasn't zoned for residential occupancy. All the tenants received notification of this, and a demand that we move in less than 2 weeks.

I filed a request for a temporary restraining order with the Malden District Court but was denied. I went to the Malden Mayor's office with it, but he said there was nothing he could do. On July 18, 2000, at 2 p.m., I was put out on the street.

Thus began my homelessness. I simply had no options. I didn't have the money to pay another rent and security deposit, especially in the middle of a month. After consulting with a local agency, I was directed to the Woods-Mullen Shelter in Boston.

I was 46 years-old, beat up mentally, physically and emotionally, and drug-addicted. I was poor, and I was vulnerable. I spent the next 3 years living mostly at Long Island Shelter, which is the sister shelter of Woods-Mullen, although, on occasion, I stayed at Woods-Mullen.

I preferred staying at Long Island because it has a lot more room than Woods-Mullen, and there's a yard where I could go outside and get some fresh air. It was at Woods-Mullen that they processed me each day for the bus ride out to Long Island Shelter.

By mid-2002, after 8 years, my concussions abated, and my brain injury healed. In early 2004, I quit all the drugs I'd been on cold turkey. I simply had had enough and finally figured out that my brain was too muddled from drugs for me to improve my lot in life. It was difficult, especially in the beginning, and I went to two AA or NA meetings a day. I had what they called post-drug addiction traumatic stress, but I stayed with it.

By the summer of 2004, a friend offered to rent me a room in her apartment, and I gratefully accepted. It was my first time off the street and out of the shelter since July 2000.

In 2006, while cleaning up the last of all the court cases I'd picked up while addicted, I temporarily lost my Social Security Disability checks. This resulted in a temporary return to Long Island Shelter for the 5 weeks it took to have the checks reinstated. Thankfully, that was the last time I needed that type of help.

Free of brain injury and concussions, past the depression, but most of all, being drug-free restored me to sanity. It allowed me to think clearly, and behave responsibly, and I've managed to live in my own home ever since.

Being homeless with nowhere to go was, in itself, a mind-numbing, stress-inducing, totally disorienting condition. In addition to the hardships that got me there, homelessness has its own set of difficulties. Every day was an exercise in killing time – and in coping – until I could return to the shelter at 4:15 p.m. I can't imagine what life would have been like had the shelters not been there.

At the Woods-Mullen and Long Island Shelters, the people who work there do many things well. A very important one is treating each and every person living there with respect and compassion. Any given day as a homeless person involves being stereotyped, shunned and disrespected. Living as a homeless person does nothing for one's self-esteem in the first place. But at the shelters, the homeless are treated as full-fledged human beings.

Were it not for such fair treatment, I'd hate to think of where my own self-confidence and sense of worth might have ended up. Without the safe-haven of the shelters, my life might have turned out very differently.

In this Thanksgiving and Christmas season, I remind everyone to be glad that the shelters are there because you never know when you might need such a place. No one is immune to adversity.

The Express Lane

At the shelter each night, rudderless by day, except for the morning visits to the methadone clinic, and breakfast and lunch at St. Francis House.

Eventually, mercifully, it's back to the shelter by 5 pm. Repeated daily, it truly grinds me down, and sucks my soul dry.

Sometimes, I go to the subway to write, or to ride out heavy rain, or the torrential hours until I can go back to the shelter. To do that, I go to unautomated stations like the North Station subway stop. There, I can apologetically pay a 1 cent fare.

At the automated stations, the fare machines don't get mad at you or disgusted; they simply don't let you ride. With a computerized fare machine, it's 0 or 1, yes or no, and without the full fare, it's always no.

Descending the steps to enter the station, I see a long line of about 15 people waiting to pay for their tokens. I'm thinking how they wouldn't be thrilled if they knew how I paid my fare.

Since I'm homeless and broke, the fare is reduced. Indeed, the rate was set at 1 penny. I assume some of the other homeless, and ne'er-do-wells, also put 1 cent into the fare box. Although I don't know how many, I do know that the 1 cent payment is for show.

The 1 cent payment is more relevant when riding the busses than on the subway. In fact, I learned the system from a bus driver on the #111 route.

When I boarded a bus, I was in the habit of simply walking past the fare box without putting any money in it. As a rule, the drivers would let it go and say nothing, but on one occasion, a driver told me to "put something in." Initially, I thought the guy was being a ball buster, but that wasn't it.

He didn't care that I rode for free; he just didn't want to hear any complaints from the other riders over it. His thinking was that by putting nothing in the fare box, I was showing the other riders that he was letting me ride for free, and he was certain to hear complaints from some of them because of it.

By putting in a penny, the riders boarding behind me, and the others already sitting down, would see me presumably paying my fare. Walking past the fare box without putting anything in calls attention to the fact that no fare is being paid. In that case, the driver's far more likely to hear complaints about why I'm riding for free when the complainant is paying full price.

The guy seemed a bit overly concerned about criticism, but who was I to grumble? He's letting me ride for a penny, and in return, he only asks that I act like I am paying full fare.

Given how down and out I'd been, acting like I was on the 'up and up' probably was good practice for the day that I, hopefully, returned to actually living on the 'up and up.'

In the end, the routine ate away at me. It was one of those things about homelessness and poverty that made me feel like a slacker or a ne'er-do-well. No matter how hard, or even how successfully, I worked at being sober and getting off the street, it never made up for the shame of it.

Her Moon Child

Her Moon Child lovingly polished
the frame cleaned the glass and
set it straight on the desk.

Admiring the old photo, he realized that
the photo – like him – was nearly all that was
left of the twenty-year-old in the picture frame.
She'd given him his life fifty-nine years earlier,
and he remembered well the young woman
in the photograph. The image was taken when she
was barely more than a teenage girl, was quite
familiar to him.

They were true pals back then;
just she and he against the world.
She had been practically his entire world,
but now she'd been gone a long time, and for good.
He would soon enough be himself,
an old man, lassoing the years until,
finally, he too, ran out of rope.

Yes, We Have No Bananas

Getting sober at forty-nine after a lifetime of substance abuse and addiction, do you suppose the picture clarifies, and life becomes rosy overnight? Of course not. Indeed, it doesn't.

One of my early mantras, when I first got sober and sane, stated, "I am fully awake and alert, and acutely aware of how screwed up my life is."

During the interminable weeks of withdrawal,

I met the challenge under the banner, "No pain, no gain – bring it on." I guess I was big on sayings.

Every once in a while, maybe every week, and at times, every few days or so, it felt like the physical ass-kicking was just going to go on and on and on.

I'd start feeling that the condition I was in, which was one of post-drug addiction traumatic stress, was never going to end. I was feeling a lot of anxiety and unease, as well as nearly complete insomnia. I also had an unnatural amount of energy, as if I could have powered a very large city had I been plugged into it.

I'd start thinking of all the months of grueling effort versus what seemed like paltry results. These thoughts made the entire enterprise of getting sober seem inequitable.

My patience started to wear thin, something like open, raw nerves rubbing on raw nerves. I had the Bobby Orr knees of frayed nerves; no cartilage, just bone grinding on bone, a psyche in need of arthroscopic surgery and rest.

Happily, it was a temporary feeling, and my mission – my jihad – was permanent.

No roses, no bananas, no parades, and no headlines about my hard work. I'm getting straight in anonymity, and there are no complaints from the partly civilized, somewhat sane, and sober me out here in the residential wilderness.

Bob's Roominghouse

If Izzy had a choice between banishing the bugs that infest this place, or the humans residing here, it would be a hard choice.

There were at least four types of flesh-eating, blood-drinking bugs at Bob's Bellingham Square roominghouse in Chelsea.

People had taken to calling them 'Bed Bugs,' and Izzy felt certain some of them were, but nobody really knew what they all were.

The humans that plagued the roominghouse were the crackheads, heroin addicts, and alcoholics who came in off the street to use the bathrooms or to congregate in small groups in the hallway by the backdoor.

They came in not to get warm or use a toilet, they mostly came in to shoot up, or to smoke their crack pipes. They seemed to be junkies and alkies of the lowest stripe and the everyday demented, criminally insane.

The rather large contingency that publicly abused substances lowered the quality of life in the roominghouse and across the city of Chelsea, especially in Bellingham Square.

The alcoholics and crackheads started drinking behind the roominghouse at 8 am, and sometimes were there all day and all night. They were especially disruptive to the tenants whose rooms faced the back alley where they congregated.

Unfortunately for those tenants, the lost souls were made more comfortable and right at home because of the abundance of milk crates available in the back alley, which they used as chairs and tables.

The bright floodlight over the backdoor provided them with ample illumination when it was dark out, and the continuous, conspicuous absence of the police only emboldened them all the more.

One girl used to arrange the crates into an elaborate makeup counter and spend hours in a crack-induced trance, picking at her face. It was pure insanity, as was much about the crack smokers.

Sometimes, the chatter of the alkies and vipers gave Izzy a headache. His room was on the first floor, and his only window faced the back alley where they hung around.

Some of the public intoxicants had big mouths and were loud. Their endless complaining and razor-sharp selfishness were fueled by their constant need for crack.

Discontent and unhappiness ruled their thoughts and their words. They hacked and spat, and grumbled throughout the day.

Izzy was continually disgusted that not one decent thought ever seemed to run through their collective minds and out of their mouths.

Without a doubt, they were a greedy, petty and contemptible group. But Izzy knew it was more than that. Izzy knew that because he was fairly new in recovery, he was particularly sensitive to their antics. Still, it didn't change the fact of their daily disruption to the quiet enjoyment of his home.

Bob himself ran them off the property a few times a day, but it didn't have any appreciable effect.

Public intoxication was epidemic in Chelsea's Bellingham Square, and the roominghouse gave the public intoxicants cover from the rest of the city and from police notice.

Then, of course, there were the other kind of bugs to contend with.

When the bugs were thick, they could nearly drive you crazy with their relentless attacks.

There were the ones you couldn't see that caused only

minor irritation until they decided to bite. When they bit, the irritation became major. They bit with a sharp pinch, like a flea. Given a night to work while you slept, they could cause scores of bites in only a few hours.

It was uncanny how they knew when you were asleep and how they could cause so much damage without waking you.

There were also bugs that were large, brown, and beetle-like but flat, that sucked on a person until they were fat and satiated with his or her blood.

If you caught one and squashed it in a paper towel, it left a fair amount of blood. But if you pinched one between your thumb and finger, they literally exploded, spraying blood over your fingers and hand.

A third type of bug was round and was either gray, black, or brown. This one seemed to be absent in the winter while playing a chief role in summer.

Izzy thought maybe these were the 'Bed Bugs', because once he put both his mattress and his box spring in plastic sleeves, they seemed to die off and disappear. Perhaps they flourished living on the mattress, and once they were deprived of that habitat, they were extinguished.

A bite from these bed bugs left what felt like a sand or glass stinger, which was quite painful. It felt as though you had a piece of glass under your skin or some kind of a sandy barb.

The bite was itchy, but if you scratched it, the skin surface would turn mushy and disintegrate, leaving a goodly sized, deep hole in the victim that, once healed, left an unmistakable scar.

When Izzy first moved into Bob's, he'd been bitten very badly until he learned how to combat the bloodsuckers. A year later, he was still annoyed as he surveyed the scars on his legs from the year-old bed bug bites.

Since Izzy had sealed his mattress and box spring in plastic sleeves, he had ceased to be bitten by any bugs except on odd occasions, usually by spiders. The plastic sleeves made life at Bob's a bit safer.

Several of the women who lived in Bob's claimed that the bugs deposited eggs underneath their skin. Although Izzy had seen no evidence of that, there were times that he'd scratched himself bloody, thinking that the bugs had indeed left something under his skin, but he never saw any evidence of eggs.

Maybe they sensed when their host was female, and seized the opportunity to bank some eggs, but on a strictly no-nonsense playing surface, that seemed a bit far-fetched. Those bugs were ultra-nasty, but, they weren't laying eggs inside people.

Another, fourth kind of bug, left a single, round bite mark or sucking hole, that was terribly itchy, and left a deep hole under the surface of the wound. It also left a scar behind when it healed.

Izzy wasn't sure what that fourth bug looked like, and he thought maybe it was merely a variation of the third type of bug.

Whenever a tenant told Bob about the bug problem, Bob's standard reply was to say that the tenant had brought them into the building. It was his way of avoiding the subject.

Izzy was 54 years old. He had lived all over and never had bugs, except for cockroaches. Bob's had cockroaches, too, but they didn't pose the problem that the bed bugs posed.

Izzy had no doubt that the bed bugs lived and thrived within the roominghouse, even though Bob claimed otherwise. To believe Bob was to believe that everyone who complained about bed bugs was guilty of bringing them into the roominghouse.

Even the wildest imagination couldn't support those numbers. Besides, Izzy knew for a fact that he certainly didn't bring any of the nasty creatures aboard.

The roominghouse was skanky, and it was easily the grubbiest and grimiest place he'd ever been in or had lived in.

As if the bugs weren't enough, there were always the addict-tenants to contend with.

Crack was the preferred drug among the tenants, the worst, subhuman bunch Izzy had ever encountered. It was they, not the bugs, that were the biggest pain in the ass.

Izzy was downright disgusted by them, and as soon as he managed a bit more income, he would quickly bid Bob's roominghouse a permanent farewell.

For the present, Bob's roominghouse certainly beat homelessness. There was nothing as bad as homelessness, as far as Izzy was concerned.

Life at the roominghouse was grungy, down and dirty, but it was ten times preferable to homeless life at Long Island or any other shelter.

Izzy kept to himself; he kept his nose to the grindstone and didn't stray from the straight and narrow path.

He tried not to be too repulsed by the varmints who lived or played at the roominghouse. Their misery was not his misery, and their lifestyle wasn't his lifestyle, he reasoned.

Even if, at one time, it had been his lifestyle, it certainly wasn't any longer. Izzy had made big changes in his life.

Izzy felt that they were a blight on the city because so much of what they did was done outdoors in public.

He referred to them as the Public Intoxicants, but it was beyond his control. He stayed busy living his own life.

When it came up, he spoke out against crack and heroin, and all the rest of it, but he wasn't militant in his actions about it. He was glad to be part of the solution and not part of the problem in the community. It was nice being on the other side of the fence for a change.

Izzy wasn't about to let the madness at Bob's roominghouse become his madness.

Meanwhile, it seemed the variety of wounds the bugs left behind on a person could be attributed not only to the type of bugs inflicting them but also how long the bugs had to work on them. People were terribly vulnerable when asleep.

These bugs lived to feed on human blood, but they weren't entirely indiscreet. When Izzy was ill with a viral infection, the bugs stopped biting him. Izzy wished there was a way to simulate a bug-deterring infection.

The most important deterrent was, without a doubt, zippering one's mattress and box spring inside of plastic sleeves. That small investment in time and money was the most powerful and effective bug interdiction that Izzy knew of.

Meanwhile, three doors down the hall in the bathroom, Izzy heard the other kind of critter that plagues the roominghouse. This one is largely responsible for the less-than-stellar reputation Chelsea carries throughout the Commonwealth as a drug town.

This is Bob's roominghouse in 2007, where the junkies come to shoot up, smoke up, and sometimes bring their tricks.

They gain entry by breaking in through the back door – a five-second chore for most – or by shouting up to a window for someone to let them in, or throw down a set of keys. Other times, they wait by the front door for someone coming home, and sneaking in behind them.

They shoot up, or smoke up, in the first-floor bathroom, which has nasty consequences for the tenants. They squirt blood on the floor or wall, leave syringes around, empty bags of dope, and generally trash the place, not to mention clogging up the toilet. That bathroom is supposed to be shared by three tenants, not half of the city.

From his room, Izzy could hear the two junkies in the bathroom discussing the syringe laws, or perhaps syringe etiquette.

"They gotta be brand new. Look at your arms… See, they ain't brand new. A friend of mine just got another year for carrying a dirty syringe. As soon as you open it, it ain't new."

"Oh, like driving a new car off the lot…"

"Yeah, right. Just like it – you're such a bean head, Jimmy."

"What're you mad about?"

"Nothing. You want a half-and-half, or a straight blowjob?"

It's a lovely dinnertime discussion for the first-floor tenants to listen to while eating their cube steak…

"You know what I want –"

"Uh-uh. Not here."

"Come on, you can – "

"I am not putting that fucking costume on in here. What if Bob comes?"

After the commotion in the bathroom, Izzy went out to the library to commit a few story ideas to paper.

The summer hours had all but killed the library in Chelsea as a writing resource, and as a result, Izzy had been going to the Revere Public Library.

Unfortunately, the Revere Library had, for

some unknown reason closed early, so Izzy returned to the bus stop for a ride home.

Walgreen's Pharmacy was next to the bus stop on Broadway, in Revere, next to the fire station. So, Izzy went in to buy some razor blades and a newspaper.

Izzy was just glad he could get something accomplished on his busted trip to write at a library computer. Besides, there was always tomorrow.

Bob, Vinnie, and Mexico

Vincent has been managing the building I live in since his grandfather, Bob, had a stroke about a month ago. Vinnie is twenty-five years old but possesses the mentality of late adolescence. He's dangerously sure of himself despite his vast inexperience, and his ongoing addiction problem. But I didn't know about that particular complication until much later.

I guess it annoyed me that Vinnie was unmindful, and certainly ungrateful of his good fortune, not that it was really any of my business. But he hadn't sacrificed or sweat for the treasure in property he was coming into. He hadn't paid any dues, and it showed; as things currently stood, he was softer than a sneaker full of shit.

Despite arrogance and bad manners, good things were coming Vinnie's way. After all, deserving isn't necessarily a condition of attainment.

To him, the wealth that arises from his family's business is just a fact of life. He'll receive it no differently than when the Tooth Fairy slipped a dollar under his pillow after he'd lost a baby tooth.

Vinnie tells everyone that he owns this building, but the truth is he manages it while his granddad is on the mend. He doesn't own it, at least not yet, but for some reason, he feels the need to tell everyone that he does. I suppose he thinks it makes him a big shot or king of the hill, but in reality, it's just more of his insecure, adolescent behavior.

His grandfather had for years looked the other way when it came to the homeless people who lived up on the roof of the Compare Market next door. They gained access to the market roof by cutting through the backyard of Bob's rooming house.

Now temporarily in charge, Vinnie wants to screw around with the status quo by cleaning out the homeless squatter's place up on the Market roof.

While the market property abuts the rooming-house property, it's separate and distinct from the rooming house and isn't Vinnie's responsibility. If the owners of the Compare Market don't mind homeless people sleeping up on their roof, Vinnie shouldn't worry about them either.

I'd rather leave those people alone, but I'm not going to sweat over it because Vinnie's going to do whatever Vinnie's going to do, regardless of what any of us think.

Still, I wish Vinnie paid more attention to some of the things his grandfather did. Bob had over forty years of operating rental properties, and Vinnie could learn a lot from him.

Every morning, Bob used to pick up day-old bread, pastries,

cakes, and pies from Stop and Shop supermarkets. He loaded up his van with the stuff and drove it to the front of the rooming house on Hawthorne Street in Chelsea.

He got there around 7:30 every morning, and parked until about 10:30, or until all of the food was gone. It was a valuable resource for his tenants and the other neighborhood residents, and he stayed parked long enough to give everyone a chance to come by and get some free food.

Then, if there was anything left, he'd drop it off at the Chelsea Salvation Army food pantry, that was just up the street.

It was a blessing to have a choice of bread, pies, and pastries that I could have for free. It helped me get by, and was sometimes the difference between eating and going hungry.

Bob's tenants, and the neighborhood people were among the poorest in Chelsea, and Chelsea was one of the poorest cities in the state.

Bob's daily routine was thoughtful and generous, and it was a way for him to give back to a city that had provided well for his family. I liked that about him, that he was willing to spend a few hours of his day delivering food to the neighborhood. Bob had followed this routine for years and helped a lot of people along the way.

Because of the stroke, Bob was totally knocked out of commission. As a result, people have had to make do without the food he brought in every day. His grandson Vinnie couldn't be bothered with helping people out, or giving back to the city. He was more interested in evicting them, and running roughshod over the homeless.

This rooming house, along with several others owned by Bob, are basically slum properties. He generated much of the family fortune by renting to the most unfortunate, and poorest folks around. But at least by bringing a van full of food for them every day, Bob made things a little better.

Rather than just another slumlord making his fortune off the poor, he was also a man who did more than his share.

Bob could be easy going and understanding with his tenants. He wasn't a fool for getting his chain pulled, but he often tolerated tenants who couldn't pay their rent, giving them extra time to pay it. He was also known to lend a few dollars.

I'm not saying he was perfect, or that he was a saint. He could be downright irascible at times, but he was a pretty decent soul who did more than most in giving back to a very poor community.

So far, Bob's grandson Vinnie had stepped into the taking role, but hadn't shown any interest in the giving back role.

The homeless people who cut through the backyard on their way to the Compare Market roof next door weren't the only trespassers using the backyard of the rooming house. It also gets used as a hangout for drinking, doing drugs and making drug deals away from prying eyes, and the police.

If Vinnie succeeds in running off the loiterers permanently, nobody will be happier about it than me. They're too loud and boisterous, and make a lousy backdrop to my home. If Vinnie's pestering inclines them to move onto greener pastures, it'll be a big improvement to our local environment and quality of life. But that's a big 'if.'

When it comes to the homeless next door, I don't understand why Vinnie's on their case. They sleep and hang out on the market roof, which isn't his property. But I do know, if he persists in trying to run them out, he's going to have a fight on his hands.

The leading squatter of the roof crew is a belligerent dope fiend named Louie, although everyone calls him 'Mexico.'

Mexico is a friend to all of the homeless addicts in the area, especially the young women. He strives to impose his style of living on the rest of the Compare Market roof community; a junkie pied piper of sorts.

Vinnie had cleaned off the market's roof of all the furniture, sleeping bags, and other junk that the illicit residents had hauled up there. He also made access to the roof far more difficult by cutting some of the tree branches, and removing a fence they had used to climb up to the low roof.

Once they got up on the low roof, they climbed up to the main roof by stacking some pieces of furniture they kept on the low roof for that purpose. But now that all the furniture had been removed, the homeless people would have to find another way onto that roof.

Vinnie and his helpers had put in a very full Sunday of work trying to eradicate the homeless people living up on the Compare Market.

Given that the market wasn't on his property, I kept wondering why he was so concerned about someone else's building.

Maybe it was because some of those same homeless people cut through his yard, and climbed over his fence to get onto the market roof.

Whatever his motivation was, it was enough for Vinnie to carry out a private little war against them.

No sooner had Vinnie cleared off the roof, and cut down the access to it, the squatters returned. They returned under the cover of darkness, and appeared to be sufficiently equipped to resume residence up on the roof.

It was beginning to look like an episode of Mad magazine's 'Spy versus Spy.'

Led by Mexico, they returned late in the night with two ladders. One was a 30-foot, yellow fiberglass ladder, the other a 20-foot aluminum ladder with red footings. Both appeared to be in good shape, if not brand new.

Since Vinnie had cut and removed a small chain link fence, and some tree branches from the rear of the property, the homeless infiltrators had no way to get over the 12-foot-high concrete wall that blocked their access to the market's property. Nonetheless, I was certain the group ringleader, Mexico, wasn't going to give up easily and without a fight.

Mexico was not my favorite person; he was aggressive and he was belligerent. He took the rule of law, and the neighborhood peace and quiet as an affront, and a challenge to his authority. He acted like our yard was his personal domain and that the rest of us, who actually lived in the rooming house, were in his way.

The fact of the matter was, he was an intoxicated trespasser who frequently disturbed the peace.

Mexico wasn't a poor, homeless man who was down on his luck, and trying desperately to survive on the streets. He worked each night at the Chelsea produce center, and earned very good money at it. He simply preferred a homeless life and spent all his money on hard drugs.

He liked playing the 'ringleader,' imposing his antagonistic presence on both the homeless crowd and the larger, overall neighborhood community, as much as he could get away with.

That first night, after Vinnie had cleared out all the homeless furniture, Mexico woke me up, bringing ladders in through the backyard. It was about midnight, when I looked out my window, to see what all the commotion was.

As I peered out, I saw Mexico carrying in the 30-foot ladder and another fellow just ahead of him lugging in the 20-footer. While I was at the window watching, Mexico whirled around to look at me, and angrily yelled out, "What?"

Given his chippie attitude, I took it to mean he thought I should mind my own business. How dare I look out my window to see who, and what, was making all the noise? But he also sounded like a spoiled child asking, 'Why can't you leave me alone?'

Apparently, he felt it was totally reasonable for them to come banging through the yard at midnight, and unreasonable of me to look out my window at the commotion. Shame on me for taking notice.

I didn't know where they got the ladders, but they were most likely stolen.

The ladders were perfect for getting them onto the market roof. The thirty-footer would get them over the twelve-foot, concrete retaining wall and then onto the lower roof. Once up on the lower roof, the twenty-foot ladder would get them up onto the big roof, which is where they got stoned, hung around, and slept at night.

The whole thing was rather on the bizarre side; I couldn't tell you why they wanted to sleep and loiter about on that roof. I suppose there is the advantage of being able to do their drugs, including using syringes, away from prying eyes.

On the other hand, they can get arrested for trespassing, or for breaking and entering. When it rains out, they're going to get wet. There's no kitchen up there, and no bathroom. It's nothing but the flat roof of a small supermarket.

The biggest reason they go up there is because they have nowhere to live, and nowhere else to go where they can shoot, pop, and smoke their drugs openly without interference.

The squatters bring up sleeping bags, chairs, and other odds and ends, but now that Vinnie's declared war on them, he's liable to keep sweeping through and throwing out all their stuff.

But Mexico is as stubborn as they come. He's not going to give up trying to have his way. As a result, there will likely be more of these late-night ladder drills in the foreseeable future.

One evening before sunset in late September, 2008, I was typing when Wendy shouted in through my open window, "Phil, your building is on fire!"

I stepped out the back door of the building, which was right next to my room's door, to see what Wendy was talking about. Sure enough, I could see flames in the window of the room directly above my room, two floors up.

I went back into my room and packed up what I needed to take with me in a backpack. I grabbed a jacket, made sure I had my meds, and my keys, and evacuated the building. Once outside, I walked around to the front of the building, to watch with everyone else as the fire department began to put out the fire.

By 11 pm, it was clear we weren't getting back into the building until at least the next day, and maybe not even then. The fire department would inspect the place for damage eventually, and determine if and when we could all go home.

Bob Rizzo set up a makeshift flop for those of us who didn't have a place to go to. It was nearby in a building he owned on 6th Street, down by the commuter rail station.

Bob set us up in an empty unit, and set out sleeping pads around the biggest room in the place. The Red Cross came by and distributed bottles of water, cots, and blankets, but since they only had a couple of cots, most of us slept on the floor on pads.

The next day, I got the word, the building was no longer fit for human habitation. The water that the firemen used to put out the blaze, was also the cause of the majority of the damage to the building.

I'd have to find a new place to call home. In the meantime, I would continue sleeping at the 6th Street flop.

When my monthly check came in a week later, during the first week of October, I rented a room in a place Bob Rizzo owned on Union Street in Lynn.

His daughter had driven me back to the burned-out rooming house to retrieve my desktop computer and other belongings.

The desktop was alright, but the keyboard to it had been ruined by water pouring down from two floors above, where the fire had been. A lot of other things like my TV, DVD player, books, and a lot of my clothing had also been ruined. So, I loaded what was salvageable into the car and took a ride to Lynn, to my new place.

The new room was large; it had a sink with running water and a fridge. The entire building was clean; there were no invading bugs, and no invading junkies shooting up in the restrooms like at the other place.

It seemed to be a quiet and orderly building. The only drawback was being on the fourth floor in a building without an elevator. But in every other way, it was a big improvement over my former digs.

Maybe the biggest problem with Vinnie, was that he was prone to bad behavior when his need to feed his addiction was aroused, which was every day.

During the fire we'd had in Chelsea, the tenants quickly evacuated. The fire chief said that once things calmed down, the tenants would be allowed to come back for their belongings, sometime during the next day.

Unfortunately, Vinnie got in there before the tenants did, and, somehow sidestepping fire department supervision, went from room to room, robbing everyone.

He stole laptops, tablets, jewelry, TVs, and anything else not nailed down, that he could convert into money for buying drugs.

As it happens, I didn't lose anything in Vinnie's string of thefts. Maybe because my desktop was scattered around my room in three pieces – tower, monitor, and keyboard – it didn't look appetizing, or maybe it wasn't even noticed. Nonetheless, I lost plenty of property due to the fire, including two televisions, VCR tapes, lots of family photographs, books, my computer keyboard, a printer, and most of my clothing.

Although Mr. Rizzo's daughter had promised some cash to help me replace my keyboard, and a few other things lost in the fire, her promises hadn't materialized. It appeared I'd be on my own when it came to replacing things until my dad called me.

Dad called to relay a message from my Uncle Paul that he had clothes for me. Obviously, Paul and Aunt Kathy had heard about the fire and were stepping up to help me out. They were a one-two punch of kindness and love, and they had my back time and again.

Although it was something of a struggle in the year since the fire, my fortunes were about to take a marked turn for the better.

My brother Matthew had become quite a success in the direct mail marketing industry. He had moved from his home in Alexandria, Virginia, to Palm Beach, Florida, and said he was going to come up north to visit me soon.

He came up to Lynn in May of 2009, helping me replace some of the clothing I'd lost in the fire. He took me to K-Mart on the Lynnway for clothing and said we were going into Boston tomorrow.

The next morning, we went to Boston to an electronics store, where he spent over a thousand bucks buying a new laptop for me. It was my first laptop, and it was a first-rate writing machine. As far as my writing was concerned, I couldn't have asked for more.

Matthew asked if I was interested in house-sitting his condo in Alexandria until he sold it, and then joined him in Palm Beach. He didn't want to leave it vacant after moving so far away.

Matthew said that once it sold, he and his wife wanted me to come down to Palm Beach, where they would find an apartment for me near their home there.

He also offered to finance the publishing of my first book, which he knew I was planning to write. Matthew had been a strong proponent of my writing from early on, and was all-in on my writing a book.

It took very little time to decide, and after about three seconds, I accepted my brother's offer. Come November, I had made the move to Alexandria, Virginia.

I had the condo all to myself rent-free, and there was nothing but time and hard work standing between me and my first book. The fire at the rooming house seemed like ancient history.

My brother wanted to keep paying the rent on my room in Lynn, so we had a fallback position should our plans not work out. So, after sending rent payments for December and January, he decided to send a check to cover three months; February, March, and April.

It made sense to stay at my old digs, when I was up in Massachusetts visiting friends, in early April.

I arrived at the rooming house, opened the front door to the building, and walked up the stairs to my room on the fourth floor. I unlocked the door to my room and walked in to find it totally empty.

My belongings weren't there. There was just a chair, an empty bureau, and a stripped-down bed. All of my possessions had been removed.

I was stunned, and wanted answers fast, but I couldn't find anyone in authority to speak to about it. There wasn't anyone around who worked there, and I couldn't find any tenants who knew anything about it, either.

I called my friends Maz and TJ, to tell them what had happened. They generously said they'd pick me up and have me stay with them during my visit. But I still had to figure out what the hell was going on at the rooming house.

Eventually, I discovered the truth about what had happened at the Lynn rooming house. I suppose I should have anticipated that Vinnie would be at the bottom of it, at the helm of the conniving thievery.

Turns out that Vinnie rifled his family's mailbox, taking Matt's 1500. Rent check, so the family simply thought I never paid the rent and had disappeared. At least, that's the story I finally got out of them.

I never did see Vinnie again, so I couldn't confront him about ripping me off, or about losing my stuff. By the time I had learned what happened, he was in prison doing time on drug charges.

I guess things just went downhill for Vinnie, that cocky lad. Things always go downhill for the user when the disease of addiction is having its way.

My brother and I got lucky on the stolen rent check, though. Vinnie never was able to cash it, so once we discovered that we stopped payment on it, and the money reverted back to Matthew's checking account.

Getting the fifteen-hundred back was a win, even if I never did get my belongings back. That was just stuff, and it all would get replaced, eventually.

Matthew sold his condo in May of 2010, and I was on my way to Palm Beach, Florida. He and his wife, Ann, were able to find a small, one-bedroom apartment for me, only five blocks from their home there. I flew down to Palm Beach and moved into my apartment on Royal Poinciana Way. My move to South Florida, by way of Alexandria, Virginia, was complete.

The plan laid out by my brother Matthew in early 2009, which we put into play in November of that year, was working out beautifully.

I had moved from a low-rent rooming house in Lynn, Massachusetts, to a one-bedroom apartment in one of the wealthiest towns in the country. It was a bit of an adjustment, and a glorious one at that.

The next order of business for me was collecting my thoughts and impressions about getting sober, and putting it all down on paper coherently, and into a readable book.

I haven't seen Vinnie or Mexico since those days in Chelsea.

Vinnie's granddad, Bob, passed away sometime after suffering a stroke.

The building that was the Chelsea rooming house before the fire, was rehabbed over an eight or ten-year period of time, into an upgraded and much nicer building than it ever had been.

I wonder if the ghosts of Wendy, John, Bob, or Jeanine, Julie, and Kim, hang out there with the rest of the Bellingham Square, Chelsea ghosts.

9-1-1 H20

Dripping with the wonderful water,

cold, cold water,

from the faucet – but from

deep in the ground –

a buried treasure, frosty cold,

the hidden asset of this rooming house,

the heat wave bringing

days and weeks of 90-degree,

high humidity transforms

this room into a furnace,

a stoking, choking, smelters dream,

but for the water, for some,

a killing dream,

I'm only 54 and, figuratively speaking,

it's killing me,

it might truly kill an octogenarian,

I feel like an 'Oven Stuffer Roaster,'

Boston tries to get folks out of their

sweatbox rooms and into air-conditioning and swimming pools,

but here in Chelsea, who knows,

but the cold water at the sink,

at the end of the hall is

blessed 9-1-1 H20,

put a pile of gold and

that faucet of water in

front of a man in the desert,

we know which he'll choose,

unless, perhaps, he has a cell phone,

in which case, he might make a call for

transport out of that desert, assuming the

carrier will accept payment in gold,

another 50 years from now,

they will, indeed, probably want

water for payment,

9-1-1 H20, 9-1-1 H20,

an easy-as-pie plan to garner

great wealth for the future,

is to store away as much fresh water

as possible today, or better yet, store it in

an area where water is already

scarce, and do it sooner rather than

later, because in the future, hoarding water will become a criminal

offense,

also, try to imagine what mobs of

thirsty people might do to get your

water, if you had chosen the

gold in the first place, you wouldn't

need to hoard water, bottom line is,

stay out of the desert,

and stay out of the future,

if you stay out of the desert,

there's no need to choose at all,

but in this global warming heat wave,

I live in a furnace of a room,

a desert of digs,

so, the best I can manage is

to stay out of the future,

which, the weatherman promises,

has more of the same:

extreme heat and humidity.

Mannequins

It was a strange experience walking through the backyard at Robbie's. Robbie and his pals had placed full-size mannequins along the driveway and backyard, that appeared to be standing around casually like real people. The first time I encountered the outlandish menagerie was at Twilight, and it really weirded me out.

Later, it was the people living there who had put the mannequins in place that proved to be truly weird, but I did finally get used to the mannequins.

However, I never did grow accustomed to the very odd people who lived there.

****

Nearly asleep, I was watching a TV ad as I was drifting off. All I remember about it, was that it was a commercial with a lot of mannequins in it. Apparently, it stirred something in my subconscious because later on, I remembered a dream I'd had about a mannequin. In the dream, I had placed a mannequin next to the door of my room in the rooming house where I lived. It seemed a normal, even clever, thing to do, at least in the dream. In fact, in the dream, the woman living next door approved and understood the humor of it. Of course, in real life, it didn't make any sense to me.

****

I had seen a similar sight in real life in Worcester in 2003. A bunch of guys living in a rooming house there had placed several full-size mannequins along their backyard walkway, which had startled me the first time I walked by them.

As fate would have it, I moved into that rooming house and learned just how weird those guys truly were.

The mannequins in the TV ad brought about my recollection of the dream about the rooming house mannequin, which in turn got me thinking about that place in Worcester with the mannequins.

I doubt that place in Worcester would have come to mind on its own. It's not a place that I would normally reflect on, given that it was such a negative experience. But the mannequin events seemed to jolt forth by association with the real-life mannequin experience I had in Worcester.

That place of Robbie's in Worcester was a thoroughly nasty shithole. I lived there for 5 months, and, amazingly, I got clean while living there, or I should say, I started getting clean while I lived there.

It took thirty months for me to get over post-drug-addiction traumatic stress, insomnia, and learning to identify and trust my instincts again. Twenty-three years of addictive drugs is a long time, and it took me nearly three years to normalize from such a long, addicted run.

One of the Worcester tenants, Ray, died just before I jumped off the methadone supertanker and out of the straightjacket of valiums and Klonopins.

His death may have been the final straw among a lot of final straws I'd had in my life then. I'd become sick to death of being a slave to the drugs, to the methadone clinic, and to my life overall.

Ray had been one of the more normal guys living at Robbie's rooming house. On a daily basis, his cooking filled the cold and cheerless house with sumptuous aromas. He was the only one of seven people who cooked anything, except for myself, and I only cooked oatmeal. I ate a lot of cereal, mostly Cheerios and oatmeal. I also bought sandwiches, subs, and pizza with the panhandling money I made. But Ray cooked serious meals, and, in doing so, provided me with the rarest of events in that grim place: a pleasurable experience, derived from the wonderful smells.

Sadly, Ray died at about 40 years old. He was a type 1 diabetic, but his heavy heroin use over the years was the main cause of his undoing. The fact that there was no heat in the house didn't help his plight.

After he died, the cops threatened to charge Robbie with some kind of murder charge if the house measured out at less than 50 degrees. But Robbie lucked out, as the place passed muster on the day they measured the temperature, but I doubt it passed by very much. It definitely was very cold in there all through the winter.

It had been a cold winter, and without heat, it was a miserably long, and shivering cold winter in that foul rooming house.

Twenty minutes after getting home, I had to either dress again for the outdoors, or stay on my bed under the covers, which is what I did most of the time.

That January, in 2004, was the coldest January on record; it certainly was the coldest I'd ever experienced, considering there was no heat inside.

The fall and winter of 2003-04, was also the most poverty-stricken I ever experienced in my life. I was hitting bottom, and the majority of the money I had was being spent buying Valium and Klonopin off the street.

My bed was a wooden door laid across the frame of an old, broken aluminum cot. I had a half-inch pad on top of the door, plenty of blankets, but not much privacy, although I had more than some people who lived there.

It was a bizarre place. There were three rooms used as bedrooms. Two of them didn't have doors, and the third was a large closet or storage space, literally under the eaves, which is where Ray lived.

There was a man who lived permanently in the living room and a woman who lived permanently in the dining room. So, the only room that could actually be used, besides one's own doorless bedroom, was the kitchen.

There were seven demented, indoor cats living there. They were wild products of inbreeding and maltreatment, that had greasy slick coats, and who pissed on everything in the house.

The cats were strange and insane, and probably never had a chance, much like the broken human beings who lived there.

The environment there probably further prompted me to make huge changes in my life. Between the miserable lifestyle I had fallen into, and the personal shame I felt about my behavior on the day that Ray died, I didn't much like the person I'd become.

There was nothing else to do but change my life and my world going forward.

Talking Jimmy Enright

Jimmy Enright was a friend of my father's and a retired railroad man when I met him in 1974. He had been all over the country working for the railroad, hooking up the engines and cars of freight trains. His true passion, however, was traditional jazz. Jimmy loved traditional jazz, and was a serious student of it. As an accomplished recordist, he had an amazing library of the live recordings he'd made in jazz clubs and venues.

Combined with the recordings he'd acquired from record shops and collectors, Jimmy had put together and curated a top-notch archive of traditional jazz, and more. But what made Jimmy's collection special, and even unique, were the recordings he made on his own equipment in the jazz clubs. Live music is the best music, and live music recorded well is a genuine treasure.

I got to see just how Jimmy recorded live bands whenever the New Black Eagles were playing at the Sticky Wicket Pub. He used a reel-to-reel deck with two microphones, one left, and one right. He set a few levels on his deck, did a soundcheck when the Black Eagles warmed up, and that was about it.

When the Black Eagles were about to begin a new set, they'd first check with Jimmy to make sure that he and his recording equipment were ready. They valued Jimmy's recordings of the band and the permanent record of their work that it represented.

Thursday nights were the best time to be at the Sticky Wicket because it was the one night the New Black Eagles played there each week.

I had the good fortune to have been at the Sticky Wicket for a number of those Thursday nights in the 1970's.

My father and Jimmy Enright were huge fans of traditional jazz, and they'd given the Black Eagles the highest of recommendations. They knew I was a music lover, and were eager to steer me in the direction of great traditional jazz. It didn't take many Thursday nights to understand why people were saying the Black Eagles were the best traditional jazz band on the planet. In fact, the New York Times is quoted as saying, "The Black Eagles are so far ahead of other traditional jazz bands, there is scarcely any basis for comparison."

The New Black Eagle Jazz Band of the 1970's was powered by leader Tony Pringle on cornet; Stan McDonald on clarinet & soprano sax; Peter Bullis on banjo; Stan Vincent on the trombone; C.H. 'Pam' Pameijer on drums; Eli Newberger on tuba; and Bob Pilsbury on piano.

The Black Eagles were the best because of the respect they held for the music, and for the genre. The individual musicians were talented, technically proficient, and even gifted. But working together as an ensemble, they were even better. They were proof positive of the proposition that the whole is greater than the sum of its parts. Their intuitiveness was keen and finely tuned, and it allowed them to mesh brilliantly as an ensemble.

Typically, one thinks of an ensemble as a supporting cast, backing up a soloist – singer or instrumentalist – in true homophonic fashion. But with traditional jazz, and in particular, with the New Black Eagle Jazz Band, that process results in a magical counterpoint, where the ensemble works simultaneously as both an ensemble unit, and as six soloists.

The Black Eagles were a well-oiled machine, and as tight as can be. They were instinctive and spontaneous, yielding undeniable and fantastic, true contrapuntal results.

As much as their individual and collective playing abilities were responsible for the success they enjoyed, it was also because they genuinely cared about the music. To them, it was very important how they presented the traditional New Orleans jazz they played.

Trombonist Stan Vincent said that in the early months of the band, the members often met just to talk about the music. They wanted to be faithful to the true, original jazz as it came out of New Orleans and, later, Chicago and New York. This required that they carefully consider what they were going to play and how they were going to play it. I can imagine many philosophical discussions ensued.

After all, they were playing a musical style that

had its beginnings three-quarters of a century earlier. It had virtually no representation within the music styles of today, so consequently, they felt it was of paramount importance to present it faithfully, keeping with the intent of the original jazz players of the early 20th century. Given the tremendous abilities the original New Black Eagle Jazz Band members had as performers and the intelligence or 'musical IQ' they possessed, they were likely destined for success. But it was the love, care, and respect they held for the music, and their willingness to get it right in terms of authenticity, that set them apart from all the other traditional jazz bands. It's their attention to detail that no others have since been willing, or able, to match.

The best Thursday night of all those Sticky Wicket Thursday nights in the 1970's was the one that fell on the Fourth of July, in 1974.

With July 4th that year falling on a Thursday, and given that it was my 20th birthday, circumstances aligned perfectly for a visit to the Sticky Wicket Pub in Hopkinton, for a birthday celebration and catching the New Black Eagle Jazz Band.

Jimmy Enright didn't record the Black Eagles every time they played at the Wicket, but he was recording the show on this holiday Thursday.

My oldest friend, Jimmy Masters, up from Virginia Beach to study at Berklee College of Music, had come with me to the Sticky Wicket. We got a ride with my father and arrived early, planning to have supper there.

Some of my other friends from Newton had been coming to hear the Black Eagles recently, but on this night, there would be a much larger than usual contingent present. Somehow, word about my birthday, and the Black Eagles playing at the Sticky Wicket Pub had gotten around.

Me and Jimmy got a table on the far side of the dining room. It was early, only 6:45, and we had just ordered a meal, and were leisurely sipping mugs of Bass Ale while waiting for our food.

By the time we had eaten, the Wicket was really filling up, and I could see some of the band members milling about the stage. Tuba player Eli Newberger and pianist Bob Pilsbury were going about their preparations, while Jimmy Enright was setting up his recording equipment at his front-row table.

Jimmy Masters and I got ourselves a table in front of the band, just to the left of Mr. Enright, while my mom and dad were sitting on Jimmy's immediate right, next to his recording equipment.

Some of the Newton people had come by the table to say 'hi,' and wish me a happy birthday. The Fourth of July crowd was buzzing, and before long, the Black Eagles would be taking the stage. They came out swinging hard, opening with an up-tempo rendition of the song, "When You and I Were Young, Maggie," banjo and drums pacing the band at Vivace.

As Tony Pringle introduced the next song, I looked beyond the band to where a number of Newton guys were sitting at two adjacent tables. They were taking delivery on a tray of frothy beer mugs, which were being handed out by my father.

Dad, to my amazement, was buying and delivering rounds to the two Newton tables. He was, without a doubt, socializing to a degree that I'd never seen from him before.

Dad was treating my friends cordially, and with a great deal of generosity. The guys appreciated it, and I did, too. I was astounded watching dad doing his best to make the night out at the Sticky Wicket Pub a huge success.

The Black Eagles were playing tight and frisky on this holiday night. With Eli Newberger providing the bottom on tuba, rather than the string bass they employed from time to time, the Black Eagles had a punchier, fuller, and more percussive sound, which I adored. They were using that sound to great advantage, and cooking with gas as they launched into Potato Head Blues.

The Sticky Wicket pub might need to batten down the hatches this night, because it looked and sounded as if the band was in the process of blowing the doors and roof right off the building.

It was fortuitous that Jimmy Enright had his reel-to-reel capturing every detail of the scintillating performance, on this most wonderful birthday night.

Jimmy himself was a wonder; he knew more about jazz bands, players, and recordings than anyone I knew. When it came to traditional jazz, Jimmy was a first-rate recordist and musicologist.

The regulars from the Sticky Wicket loved him, and he was particularly well-respected by the traditional jazz crowd that poured into the Wicket on Thursdays.

The band treated him deferentially as an insider. If I wanted to hear something in particular, I'd ask Jimmy to pass along my request to the band, and it wouldn't be too long before they played it.

For the Black Eagles, Jimmy was something of a public relations man, in addition to being a documentarian of their music. Jimmy loved the music the Black Eagles played, and he loved being a part of it, even if only in a modest way.

Within a couple of days of the July 4th get-together, I had a 90-minute cassette recording of the Black Eagles from that night that Jimmy recorded. He had recorded the music on his reel-to-reel, and transferred it onto a cassette for me.

Jimmy was a very thoughtful and generous man. He loved traditional jazz, and he loved live music, almost as much as he loved people. He was a true gentleman with a lot of class.

With much of the evening of music still ahead on that July 4th night and surrounded by family and friends at age twenty, I don't believe I realized that things were as good, and about as perfect, as things can get. I didn't know how lucky I was. But I was just twenty then, and what does anyone know when they are twenty?

It's Not Called 'Dixieland' Jazz

I was a young boy when I first heard traditional New Orleans jazz music, spilling out of my father's silver Wollensak reel-to-reel tape deck.

Unlike much of the music that my mom and dad listened to – which I thought was schmaltzy – this music cooked. It didn't plod along, mired in an unchanging, syrupy groove that was overly simplistic and far too sweet. This traditional jazz music was a different animal.

It was kaleidoscopic and dynamic, jumping and moving, driving and exploding, at times marching in a singular mission and at other times scurrying in multiple, galloping, divergent directions in joyous, intelligent syncopation. It reminded me of the aural assembling, disassembling and reassembling of a Chinese puzzle.

Each song was an adventure, a grand excursion leaving home, exploring new terrain, and returning home safely. The variety of instrumentation and the virtuosity afforded each was striking to my youthful ears.

It was physically and intellectually satisfying and stimulating to me that so many separate musical lines could coexist and make sense, furthermore combining to create such an articulate whole. It was my first contact with contrapuntal music, and my first sample of improvisation.

My mom didn't listen to jazz – it seemed most people did not – and most of the time, dad listened alone, except when he sat out on the front stairs or in the den with Fred 'Red' White.

Mr. White was my friend Michael's dad, and he was crazy about jazz. They lived four houses down from us on Norland Street in the Orchards of East Holliston, MA. On summer days, he and my dad could be found in the late afternoons or early evenings sitting out on the White's front steps listening to jazz.

He seemed to know a lot about New Orleans's traditional jazz music, and he spoke very passionately and authoritatively about it and of the men who performed it. He seemed to know every bit as much about it as Dad did, which was saying something because Dad was well versed and, in fact, could play the heck out of the licorice stick – the clarinet – and the saxophone.

They would sit out on the White's front stairs, Red always in his dark green work pants, on summer evenings or Saturday afternoons, listening to that most American of music, New Orleans traditional jazz.

They'd tune into a jazz show on the radio or play one of Dad's many reel-to-reel jazz tapes on the Wollensak.

I might go fishing as they listened and talked about jazz, return hours later, and they'd still be on the stairs listening to jazz with the same enthusiasm as earlier.

It was plain to see they loved that music and loved talking about it – describing it, and relating bits of trivia about it to each other. For me, it represented one of the rare, endearing postures of my father from my childhood years. I really liked him when he listened to jazz.

Not surprisingly, music and jazz music, are things we agree on and share today.

I was too young to fully embrace it, but there was a magical quality to the trumpets and clarinets, trombones, drums, piano, and tuba as the music softly wafted across the summer nights.

As the music carried across the night air, the elements played upon it, causing it to swirl; the sound stretched and shortened, dipped and turned, as music outdoors will. Somehow, it merely added to the majesty and the mystery of this music that was already far different than any other.

It was notable to me that in traditional jazz, there was almost never any singing involved. It was just the players on their instruments. Until now, almost all of the music I'd heard was homophonic, that is, comprised of a band playing as a supporting unit for a singer or singers.

Except for the classical pieces I played in the school orchestra or occasionally heard on the radio, jazz was the first instrumental music I'd encountered. It was quite different from the classical stuff and much more exciting. It seemed freer than anything I'd heard.

The pure instrumental nature of it necessitated a different kind of musical storytelling, giving it a different musical personality altogether. It was one that I could discern and appreciate.

The Wollensak produced a tinny, trebly sound, and was inferior compared to today's systems, but it sounded superb to me, and it more than did the job.

Whenever a discussion of traditional jazz broke out, Dad would always inform all parties that the term 'Dixieland' jazz was incorrect. New Orleans or traditional jazz was the correct and accurate term and should always be employed over the dreaded misnomer, 'Dixieland.'

He maintained that there were those who were insulted by the term 'Dixieland' jazz.

To this day, forty-five years later, Dad still likes to point out that the term 'Dixieland' jazz is incorrect. So it is, and so he does.

I first started to listen seriously to jazz, including traditional New Orleans jazz, in my mid-teens.

My 20th birthday was celebrated at the Sticky Wicket Pub in Hopkinton, MA, which was then the home of the New Black Eagles Jazz Band.

The New Black Eagles were a kick-ass traditional New Orleans jazz band that had deservedly achieved a fair amount of notoriety in the Boston area and, indeed, around the world in the 1970's.

Known as the 'New' Black Eagles, they took their name from the original New Orleans jazz band, the Black Eagles, which they emulated, out of respect and admiration.

I took them in at the Sticky Wicket Pub frequently in the mid-1970's with my dad, my mom, who'd become a fan, and some of my friends.

Thanks to the late Jimmy Enright – a dedicated jazz recordist, musicologist, and family friend – some terrific recordings of the New Black Eagles at the Sticky Wicket Pub exist. Those live recordings go well with the LP's the band recorded in the studio, although, as my old teacher, Professor Dyer, used to say, there is no music as good as live music.

Mr. White and my dad spoke with enthusiasm, great admiration, affection, and warmth about the men who performed in the various jazz bands.

It seemed that many of the musicians were colorful people with colorful names, and even the jargon itself was colorful:

"That Bix – *and he only lived to be 27,"* or *"Listen to* Satchmo *hit those* rifle shots!*"*

"Back in the days of The Hot Five *and* Hot Seven, Armstrong *used a coronet; like a slugger going to a lighter bat later in his*

career, Louie only used the trumpet later on. The coronet is a young man's instrument; it takes a lot of wind. Try flutter-tonguing *with a coronet."*

"I love the Benny Goodman Quartet – Krupa *slamming the* rim shots, Wilson *is smooth on the* horseteeth, Lionel Hampton's *magical mallets,* Harry James *knocking down the walls of Jericho, and* Benny *on the* Licorice stick *with* chops suey deluxe!"

The jazz musicians were a fascinating bunch to me. They seemed at the same time heroic and tragic, and very cool.

To be at the center of that great music had to be akin to having the world on a string. Surely, anyone who could play like that must have been a couple of steps closer to Heaven. And if you can play music like that, what else would you need?

I studied music at Boston State College and the New England Conservatory, but my education actually began back in the 1960's when I was a young boy.

Listening to Dad's traditional jazz, and to Red White and Dad discussing it was how I first obtained my sweet tooth for jazz.

The jazz was magical and intelligent, and it elicited a powerful, spiritual passion in me from the start. The spontaneity and abandon inherent in it grabbed me instantly.

New Orleans traditional jazz was for me love at first listen, and it's remained an element of joy throughout my life. It's a superior form of communication and I'm thankful that I had an early introduction to it. Just don't call it 'Dixieland' Jazz!

Snippets No. 1:
Connie's Clatter

"I'm from the 70's,
not from the 60's."

"That's a good year."

"And I'm fine."

"But you ain't no woman. You're a man
trying to be a woman."

"You come get some of this fine, good
stuff, and I'll *show* you a woman."

"Fuck you, you drizzly, drizzly ass. I'll
show you who's a woman."

"Bad day! I broke my last cigarette when I was
lighting it."

"I wish I had a last cigarette."

"Ya, well, we'll get cigarettes later. Right?"

"My mother had a heart attack, a stroke. She's
on kidney medicine. She's only sending me $400 a month."

"What'd she have, a heart attack or a stroke?"

"Both, I guess."

"Oh, man, what a drag!"

"No kidding. I need my money, even if it's only 400. Her being in the hospital might screw it all up for me."

"Your problems always take the freaking cake, Connie."

"I can't sell enough Percocets to buy the Klonopins I need, so I need that money from my mother, for fuck's sake."

"You sure about that?"

"You fuckin' drizzly ass! Yeah, I'm sure, okay? That's why I need that fuckin' money."

"Maybe you could take less of them…"

"What – are you alright? To hell with that; I can handle it."

"You can handle it…"

"What? Ya, I can handle it. Okay?"

"Okay."

"After I get my pins, we'll get cigarettes."

"How we gonna do that?"

"Don't worry about it."

"How are we gonna get cigs after you buy your

Klonopins? I want to know."

"What do you mean? I'll get 'em from the chink in Dorchester. I'll trade him for food stamps."

"He still takes them?"

"Yes, he still takes food stamps for stuff."

"You conning me, Connie?"

"Drizzly ass. Yes, for fuck's sake. He takes them. Look, go get your own if you don't like it."

Snippets No. 2:

Bullshitting in Bellingham Square

"I was hitching from South Carolina to go on leave. A state cop stopped me and said, 'What are you doing on my highway?'"

"I was going to say I was going home to Boston, that I was on leave, but as soon as I opened my mouth, he said, 'Oh jeez, I got me a Yankee nigger-lover, Jew-lover.'"

"He wrote me a ticket and scared me shitless."

"When I was in airborne school in South Carolina, I had a sergeant who had grown up near the base. He was from practically next door. The guy loved me. He once said to me, 'You got the balls of a lion whose ass is on fire.' I couldn't do any wrong in this sergeant's mind, ever since I solved a problem he was having with one of the soldiers. He wanted this guy taken down a peg, so I sucker-punched him and broke his nose. I took care of his problem, and he took care of me after that. Easy duty, choice assignments."

"He called you a nigger lover, Charlie, but when I was living with a girl in South Carolina, the locals called me 'nigger.'"

"Well, ya, Jim, you're black, but I'm not, so I guess that was the best he could come up with."

"I guess that's true, Charlie."

"My niece's two boys are mulatto. They were out in their neighborhood in Winchester, walking two little Pekinese. Some lady from across the street called the police and told them there were two black boys walking attack dogs on her street," recounted Charlie.

"I remember when I lived down south, some people called a black and white couple 'salt and pepper.'"

"Not when I lived with a white girl in South Carolina, Izzy, then they called me nigger."

"People really called you that to your face?"

"Yeah, they did, Missy. By the way, are you still on the methadone program?"

"Yup. I'm coming down 5 milligrams a day. I was on 200 mg."

"To me, the whole ballgame really starts when you get down to zero milligrams. Once you're down to zero, you have to learn how to live straight."

"I was on 200 milligrams, but I'm down to 35 milligrams now."

"That's fantastic, Missy."

"Yeah, nice going."

"Thanks, Charlie, thank you, Jim."

I wasn't sure I believed her. Coming down 165 milligrams at 5 milligrams a day is an incredibly rapid pace. I don't know if they'd allow it unless it were a mandatory detox due to a disciplinary discharge.

I liked Missy, she was a good person. Whether she chose to detox off the methadone at 5 milligrams a day or was being mandatorily detoxed didn't much matter. Missy would get sober when she was ready. Sadly, within a couple of months, Missy was dead from an overdose.

Sometimes, the grim reaper of overdose gets ready sooner than the soul gets ready for sobriety.

It Could Have Been Future Me

Chase came walking up to the Mass Ave bench I was sitting on. It was my last bench of the day before the shelter reopened.

He looked rough, shaky, and too white. Since he had chosen to share his presence with me, I thought I'd focus on someone else's misery rather than my own.

It was a bit like déjà vu. Apparently, we shared some of the same experiences, and in some cases, the similarity was striking.

Chase is probably sixty years old if he's a day. He said he lost his social security checks and didn't know why.

I replied that they'll squash you like a bug if you give them half a chance. But it's also true that when they shut you off, they always have a reason and will tell you that reason in a letter. If you're not getting mail for some reason, they'll tell you in person or even on the phone, so long as you prove who you are.

He repeated that he had lost his social security checks and that he didn't know why he lost them. But it sounded dubious, at best, to me. How could he not know?

He also said that he had obtained housing and that he had lost that, too, before he had even moved in. In this instance, he did know why he'd lost it. He said that the Boston Housing Authority told him he had a bad attitude, which was one contention of his that wasn't hard to believe. He did have a piss-poor attitude, and he was a complainer.

Next, Chase said that he was eating only one meal per week because he refused to use the shelter restrooms. He said he also refused to use the public restrooms that are all over the city.

It was then that I realized that Chase had significant mental health issues.

In fact, Chase wasn't using the shelters, period. He said that he was safer in the woods, which wasn't true at all, of course.

He then said that he was really sick, dope sick, and that his pain medication had been stolen.

I ventured a wild guess, asking him if he were on opiate pain meds. He said yes, he was on morphine and Percocet's.

I figured he had an addiction problem by the manner in which he told me he was on morphine and percs. He informed me far too casually, like someone who talks about drugs fondly and frequently.

Anticipating that he had tried or was going to try to get the pills replaced, I asked him if he'd gotten a police report of the theft. He said that he hadn't and also that he had already tried to get them replaced without success.

Drug addicts pull this on doctors and hospitals all the time. Getting a second chance is rare; cries of lost pain pills almost always fall on deaf ears.

A police report verifying that a theft had occurred can make a difference to the prescribing doctor, but not always.

Chase had pain issues, he said, but that's an old and somewhat irrelevant story because his addiction is so much more impactful and immediate than his pain considerations. Plus, Chase had many other problems – the most fundamental and serious being his mental health.

Chase was by now understanding that I wasn't a layperson and that he couldn't bullshit a bullshitter. This saved me from having to listen to him elaborate on his pain issues and also demonstrated to me that he wasn't totally crazy.

I'd been lending him a patient ear of sympathy, and when we both got onto the Mass Ave bus to go our separate ways, I gave him three pieces of advice, things I did when I was sort of like him.

I had been addicted to drugs very much like he is. I got off them and recommended to Chase that he get off them, too. No tricks, no secret methods, just quit them.

I had lost my social security checks, the same as him. So, I cleaned up the warrants that were out on me, that had caused me to lose them. Unfortunately for me, as soon as my landlady knew I'd lost them, she put me out.

She wasn't going to wait six weeks for her money. I don't hold her at fault; it was entirely her prerogative, but it was a bit cold.

It takes six weeks to get social security checks reinstated, but once I do, I can get back to living normally, in a rooming house or an apartment.

Whatever caused him to lose his social security checks, I told him he needed to fix it. Just like kicking all the drugs, it won't be painless.

There's always a price to pay. Getting my checks reinstated was hard, first because I had to surrender to three different court systems to get my warrants quashed, and that resulted in about six weeks in jail, getting it all settled. Secondly, it's causing me to be back at this homeless shelter for another six weeks, and I can think of better places I'd rather be. Simply put, it was absolutely something that I had to do.

Finally, don't look at the whole mountain of problems all at once; simply address them one at a time. You don't have to see the entire staircase. Just take the first step, which is what Martin Luther King, Jr. recommended.

I know that people in his position often get advice, but because their position feels hopeless, they rationalize by believing the advice is a lot of bullshit. Nonetheless, I concluded by saying to Chase, "Try it. My life is good."

And I couldn't believe my ears. It really is good, which is extraordinary.

A Broken Neck and Halo Brace

I worked refinishing wooden doors and kitchen cabinets at a condo conversion project in Boston in 1981. The project was on Commonwealth Court, just off Commonwealth Avenue in Brighton.

Condos were a big seller then, and as the latest real estate trend, buildings that had rented apartments for decades were now renovating the units and selling them individually as condos or condominiums.

When work was over, I headed to my second job, playing drums in a rock band. Most nights of the week, the band either played at a club or we took advantage of a night off by rehearsing.

It was Friday, October 9th, 1981, and it was payday. My boss, Leon, was going out with my sister, which is how I connected with the job.

Leon was roughly my age, 27, give or take a year or two. He was in charge of getting all the doors and kitchen cabinets refinished and all of the units painted throughout the condo project.

I was the only one on the project who was refinishing doors and cabinets, so there was plenty of work for me. Leon also had a crew of four painters who were painting all of the approximately 40 units.

The painters were all from South Boston, and although they kept to themselves, I got along alright with the crew chief, as well as with the other guys. But for some reason, they didn't have much regard for Leon, although I couldn't say why.

I had only been on the job for a few weeks at this point, so whatever the reason was for the general animosity between the painters and Leon, it was beyond me.

Leon was an Israeli citizen, and a veteran of two wars, which is why it was so surprising the way things turned out that afternoon.

5 pm was quitting time, so by 4:30 pm; I was packing up the tools and getting my stuff together to bring over to where Leon was parked. All that was left to do for the day was pick up my paycheck.

The painters had come over to Leon also, presumably to get paid. I didn't know what was going on between Leon and the painters, but the crew chief and Leon started to have words. It had something to do with money, getting paid, or both.

Leon was bigger than the kid from Southie, and as a veteran of two Israeli wars, I figured he could handle himself more than adequately. However, in practice – at least in this instance – that proved not to be the case.

Their disagreement came to blows, and the fight was brief but intense. The Southie painter hit Leon with 5 or 6 solid punches to the face in rapid succession, and that was the end of it. Leon was down, and the fight was over.

Once the crew chief had dispatched Leon, his three friends started to move in on me. They were licking their chops at the prospect of kicking my face in. Fortunately, before anything happened, the crew chief waved them off. The painters withdrew, and my beatdown was off the table, leaving just Leon and myself in the gloaming.

Leon was a mess. His face was a mass of welts and cuts. It was already badly swollen, and I think he was somewhat in shock.

Leon was in no way ready for the kid from South Boston. For the most part, young men from Southie knew well how to fight, were good at it, and in many cases enjoyed it. Besides that, I learned also that Leon had been fasting for the past two days in observance of Yom Kippur. Who knows how much the fasting had zapped his strength and stamina?

He asked me if I'd drive him to the hospital, and of course, I did.

I helped him into the passenger seat of his Volkswagen bus, got behind the wheel, and drove him to St. Elizabeth's Hospital.

The X-raysshowed that Leon had four broken bones in his face. They were admitting him to treat the fractures and make certain there were no complications from concussion or blood clots.

I've never seen a fight where someone received so much damage from so few punches so quickly. Later, I wondered if maybe the Southie painter had been using brass knuckles or a roll of quarters in his fist to have caused so much damage, but I never saw anything suspicious that day.

Leon asked if I'd drive his VW home and keep it over the weekend. On Monday morning, he wanted me to take it back to Boston to the job site and hand out the paychecks.

The paychecks were still in the VW's glove compartment and never got handed out because of the fight and Leon's subsequent injuries.

Monday was Columbus Day, and I arrived at the work site at around 7 am. I got the paychecks out of the glove box and went to find the painters to pay them.

Leon wasn't back to work yet, as planned, but I expected he'd be in on Tuesday or Wednesday.

The band I played in, The Marginals, had rehearsal that night, so after I knocked off at 5 pm, I went to the El Phoenix for supper. I wanted to eat nearby since rehearsal was just up the street in Kenmore Square. Besides, the Phoenix had great Mexican food and was renowned for it.

After I ate, I drove to Kenmore Square and parked next to the building where the band had a rehearsal room. It was barely a block from Fenway Park, sitting just at the bridge that crosses over the Mass Turnpike on Brookline Ave.

The rest of the band had shown up by 7 pm, and we got in about 3 ½ hours of rehearsal time before knocking off at 10:30 pm.

Before breaking up for the night and going our separate ways, we all went across the street to the Rat, or Rathskeller, to look in on our competition. The lead guitarist in our band, Alan, and my brother Mark, who was our bassist, often went into the Rathskeller after rehearsal. They liked to check out the local punk and new wave bands that were playing there to see how they measured up.

I rarely went into the Rat, and when I did,

I stayed just long enough for a short glass of Pickwick Ale. Unlike the other guys in the band,

I was married. I had a wife and a young son at

home in Malden.

I started the day early, refinishing doors and kitchen cabinets from 7 am to 5 pm. After quitting time, I'd have supper somewhere and then go back to work drumming with the band.

If we were performing, we worked until 1 or 2 am, and if we were rehearsing, we knocked off at 11. Our rehearsal building had an 11 pm cut-off time for the bands.

So, while Alan and Mark hung out at the Rat to see the bands, I was more interested in wetting my whistle with a beer and going home.

One thing that I liked about the Rat, was they had Pickwick ale on tap. It was a tasty red ale that I'd never seen on tap anywhere else.

Being a Monday night, the Rat was quiet, and it was easy to find a table. I was nursing my ale and listening to the band with the guys.

To me, the band seemed like most of the punk and new wave bands I'd see in the Boston clubs; poor musicianship and an amateurish approach were the prominent traits. Occasionally, a band would prove to be an exception, revealing capable chops or interesting material. But try as I might, I could never find any punk bands that I truly liked.

I had finished my ale, and it was time to go home. So, I said my goodbyes and headed out into what was left of the Columbus Day night.

As I made my way over to where I'd parked the VW bus, I was looking forward to driving my own vehicle again. Hopefully, Leon has begun healing enough to pick up his VW tomorrow.

Heading home, I always drove through Kenmore Square, cut over to Storrow Drive, taking it through the Copley Square tunnel down to Leverette Circle, and from there, picking up Route 93 north to Malden.

Traffic was a bit heavier than usual for 11:15 at night, maybe because of the holiday.

As I entered the Copley Square tunnel, I shifted into third gear to keep pace with the rest of the traffic.

Just before I reached the end of the tunnel, there was a tremendous explosion. The driver's side rear tire blew out and kicked the VW over a couple of feet to the left. This put the two driver's side wheels up on the high curb that lines the tunnel, setting the VW at a sudden, abrupt angle.

Attempting to keep it under control, I drove it off the curb and fully back onto the street. But being up on the curb and then down again started the van rocking from side to side, and the rear tire being flat added to the instability.

Just as I emerged from the Copley Square tunnel, a few short seconds after the van had started rocking, it flipped over and rolled. When the VW finally stopped rolling, I was upright again, still in the driver's seat, and hands on the steering wheel despite not wearing a seatbelt.

I ended up about 100 feet up the road from the tunnel's exit and sitting sideways across Storrow Drive, blocking the lanes. I got worried that a car coming out of the tunnel was going to broadside me, so I decided I'd better get out of the van pronto and off the road.

The driver's door wouldn't open, so I got into the passenger seat and tried the passenger door, which, fortunately, did open. I got out of the van and hurried over to the side of the road; then, I stepped over the guardrail to get completely out of harm's way. Storrow Drive, particularly at night, is no place for pedestrians.

Cars couldn't get by the VW, and traffic started to back up. One car, a sports car, squeezed past the VW, and as he drove by shouted over to me that he'd call for help as he drove off.

Having a chance to see the VW and assess its condition from the safety of the roadside, I could see that all the glass windows that wrapped entirely around the van were smashed, and all four tires were flattened. The van appeared to have been in one hell of a wreck, and apparently, so had I.

Almost miraculously, I seemed uninjured. The only exception was that it felt like I might have thrown my back a bit out of whack, which happens to me once in a while. But if I did, it was minor, and I didn't have a single scratch on me to boot.

Within a matter of minutes – even faster than if the motorist had summoned them – an ambulance showed up.

The EMTs began checking me out and asking questions. They wanted to bring me up the street to Mass. General Hospital, but I told them no thanks. I was waiting for the tow truck and then taking a cab home to Malden.

The two EMTs continued trying to convince me to get checked out at the hospital, but I had made up my mind that once the VW got towed away, I was going home. I felt alright and didn't think there was any reason to go to the hospital.

But, the EMTs kept on me, citing chapter and verse of what could be broken and what could go wrong. Finally, I reversed the field and agreed to go to MGH and get checked out.

The first order of business was they laid me on a wooden board and put my neck in some kind of elaborate, square-shaped brace made of a hard rubber-like substance.

Next, they used wide strips of white medical adhesive tape across my forehead that were taped down to the board on either side of my head, to further immobilize my neck. These guys were determined to get me to the hospital safely and without any further complications.

The tow truck arrived, and they started to get the VW up onto the back of the wrecker just as the EMTs were getting me into the ambulance. They got my stretcher locked into place, and we started our drive to the Mass. General Hospital.

It was after midnight by the time I arrived at the MGH emergency room. I got triaged and registered, and then the long process of X-rays began. Over the next couple of hours, I had an enormous number of X-rays taken. Most of them were taken with me, holding sandbags in each hand.

Holding the weight of the sandbags pulled my shoulders down so they could get a clear X-ray of my cervical spine area. Apparently, the c-spine is a difficult area to get a clear x-ray of.

By pulling the shoulders and the collar bones down with the sandbags, the cervical spine is better exposed, improving the x-ray views.

I had to wonder, though, if I wasn't getting too much radiation from the several dozen X-rays they took. I didn't want to start glowing in the dark if it could be helped.

By 3:30 am, they were done taking x-rays, and I was waiting for the doctor who was going to read them and determine what needed to be done.

I was waiting in the doctor's lounge or coffee room. It was much nicer than your average hospital waiting room. There was a half-dozen doctors on break at the time. I had been invited to wait in there when I had gotten back from radiology.

While I was waiting, I saw a stack of my X-rays on the table next to me. I picked them up and started leafing through them.

I dropped one of the X-rays on the floor, then bent over and reached down to pick it up. As I was retrieving it, the ER doctor assigned to me was just entering the room. He shouted, chastising all of the doctors there, saying something like, "What are you doing letting this patient with the broken neck bend over like that?"

Nobody said anything; I wasn't their patient, and I doubt they knew anything about me, so it was an odd moment.

The ER doctor informed me that I had a broken neck. He explained it was an acute fracture of C-6, a fracture of C-7, and 3 mm of anterior subluxation, meaning that those three vertebrae had been knocked out of alignment.

I could hardly believe I had a 'broken neck.' I wasn't really in pain, and I wasn't paralyzed. But as I went on about it, the doctor actually got rather annoyed at my disbelief and at my assertions of feeling pretty good.

It was only a matter of time, however, before my feeling pretty good was going to change.

The ER doctor said I was going to be admitted. He said an orderly was going to wheel me down to a triage room where I would wait to be admitted.

I had the orderly take me to a phone where I could call my wife to let her know what was going on. I told her I was at the MGH and that I had a broken neck, and they were admitting me.

She said to me, "I thought you died when you broke your neck…" I was tempted to make a wisecrack but thought better of it.

I said that I'd heard that, too, but the fact was, I had one. I could hear in her voice that she was a bit shaken up by the news. I said I'd call her later, when I had all the admitting information, not to worry, and to go back to bed.

The orderly wheeled me to a triage room to wait to be admitted and then went off, presumably to transport another patient.

An hour later, a nurse came in and wheeled me to the hallway just outside the triage room I'd been in. I was being cued up in line for admitting.

A bit after I'd been dropped off by the orderly, I started feeling some pain in my neck. I didn't know what it was, only that I felt a burning pain in my neck, and it was definitely increasing.

I told the nurse about the pain and that it was getting more intense as we spoke. I also told her that I hadn't had any pain medication yet. She said she'd get me a Percocet and a cup of water, which she brought back to me in a couple of minutes.

They were finally admitting me at 5:30 in the morning. They asked me about pain, and I told them it was pretty bad and getting worse. I hadn't had any pain over the first four hours, but it was coming on like gangbusters now.

The triage nurse had given me a Percocet on two different occasions over the last 75 minutes, but it wasn't touching the intense, burning pain that was in my lower neck.

A little while after I'd been given a bed in a room with three other men, a doctor came in to address my pain medication. He explained that he was starting me with an injection of Demerol every six hours and then administered the first injection before he trundled off.

Next on the agenda was a visit to the brace shop, where they'd fit me for a temporary neck brace. They decided on a clunky, metal job. It was heavy, and it kept my chin up a bit more than was entirely comfortable. But since I'd only be wearing it for a few days, it was easy to put up with.

The pain I was having in my neck over the last hour before my next shot was a real bitch. As it played out, the Demerol injections were only doing the job of painkilling for five hours instead of six.

After squirming and fidgeting in pain for an hour before each Demerol injection, I addressed the matter with the pain doctor. He simply changed the routine to an injection of morphine every eight hours instead of Demerol every six, and that took care of the problem. In fact, on the morphine, I was as high as a Georgia pine and certainly feeling no pain.

On late Tuesday afternoon, on my first full day in the hospital, I met the surgeon who had my case, Dr. Michael Joyce. He was a young guy who seemed fairly easygoing but spoke with authority and confidence. He had a good bedside manner and conveyed some of his calm and confidence to me.

Dr. Joyce was very good at explaining the elements of my injury, and he used a chalkboard to illustrate what he was describing. He diagrammed my cervical spine and the problems with it due to the fractures and subluxation.

He said my neck would be corrected by doing a 'cervical fusion' on it. He explained that they would fuse my cervical spine from C-5 to C-7.

Dr. Joyce said they would use pieces of bone sawed off my pelvic crest to facilitate the fusion. They implant pieces of bone between C-5 and C-6 and between C-6 and C-7. Once the bone grafts fuse, which takes a number of weeks, my c-spine would be whole and stable again.

Initially, they glued the pieces of bone in place. To keep it straight and in place until the bone grafts take hold, they drill a small hole in C-5 and another in C-7. Then they run a piece of 18-gauge stainless-steel wire through the hole in C-5, run it down and through the hole in C-7, then back up to C-5, where they tie it off in a square knot, using the two ends of the wire.

Between the sawing and drilling, the glue, and the steel wire, it all sounded like construction work or mini-carpentry.

Dr. Joyce said I'd be going in for surgery this coming Friday morning, the 16th, at 7 am. So, I had just three days to wait.

In the meantime, I had some visitors to help me pass the time. The very first visitor I had was my boss, Leon. I thought maybe he was feeling a bit guilty for having me drive a van that had baloney skins for tires, causing the blowout and my broken neck. But I should have known better.

Incredibly, it turned out he was there to ask me for four hundred dollars. He had a four-hundred-dollar deductible on his auto insurance, and the asshole was asking me to pay it. I thought I had heard everything, but this took the cake. It certainly showed, without any doubt, that Leon was a clueless moron.

His request has to be one of the biggest miscalculations of all time. It was easier now to understand how things between Leon and the painter from Southie got to where they did. His capacity for insulting a person was bottomless.

Upon reflection, I would like to have said something clever and cutting to the dipshit, but at the time, I was so stunned by his request I only answered in the simple negative. I didn't have four hundred dollars, and if I did, I definitely wouldn't have given it to him under those circumstances. If any money was changing hands, it was coming in my direction.

Leon left after five minutes, and I don't think we ever spoke again. His being there was somewhat dreamlike, but that was often the norm during my stay at MGH while I was on the morphine. I was usually as high as a kite, and a lot of the time, I was in a dreamlike state.

Sometimes, when the morphine had me high as shit, I'd lose my sense of up and down. Lying in my hospital bed and looking at the nurses and doctors coming and going, it looked as if they were walking on the ceiling. I know it's a strange thing to say, but that's how it looked.

After a while in that state, with its upside-down, trippy effect, I'd begin to get a little confused and a little scared. It was almost like when I had too much to drink and got the spins. It felt like gravity wanted to pull me down.

To remedy the entire ordeal, I deduced that if I took a glass of water from my bed tray and emptied some of it out, whichever way the water went had to be down.

So, I'd grab a cup of water and pour the contents out. As soon as the water spilled out, heading for the floor, my entire sense of direction, especially up and down, snapped back into correctness. It was a relief; everything was once again exactly right; up was up, and down was down.

It's remarkable how real the mixed-up sense of up and down felt. But my logical brain was working fairly well, and it was telling me that things couldn't actually be as they seemed.

Although I'd done a lot of drugs in my time, morphine wasn't one of them. It was a lot different than heroin, even though heroin is derived from morphine.

What the morphine had that the heroin does not have is the element of a hallucinogen and a tendency to put the user in a very dreamy state.

I smoked John Players Navy Cut cigarettes in those days, which was a strong, non-filter cigarette.

Because I was so heavily medicated, I tried to be careful when I was smoking.

They were giving me Valium to help control the muscle spasms in my neck. So, between the morphine and the Valium, I frequently nodded out, and sometimes the nod turned into a nap.

Whenever I woke up, the first thing I always wanted was a cigarette. But every time I went to light up, I could never find any matches.

It turned out the nurses were taking away my matches whenever I started to nod out. They were afraid I'd start a fire in the bed or burn myself. But at least when I awoke, they always gave the matches back to me.

The night before the surgery, Thursday night, the surgeon came by to get me. He led me to just past the ward I was in, to where he had an office.

He wanted to go over the routine for the morning and once again illustrate on a large grease board how the surgery would proceed.

He wanted to be certain that I was fully versed about the procedure, which I was, and that I had no questions and no unnecessary anxiety.

He said an orderly would come by to get me at 7:00 am and bring me down to the operating room. He walked me back to my room and bid me adieu. Everything but the surgery had been done, and tomorrow morning, we'd close the deal.

The orderly came by as planned at 7:00 am and brought me down to just outside the operating room, where the anesthesiology staff began sedating me in preparation for the surgery.

First, they said they were giving me Valium for starters. I forget how much they gave me, but I do remember that it was a lot.

They inserted an IV line in my arm and rolled me into the operating room. They moved me off the gurney and onto the operating table. The next and last thing I recall is they had me sucking on a thick stick of a white, mint-flavored substance that was numbing my mouth and my throat.

The Valium was knocking me down, and together with whatever else they'd given me, I was under in a snap.

I woke up at 1:30 in the afternoon in the Post Anesthesia Care Unit (PACU), or recovery room.

I looked up to see my father sitting next to me, keeping watch. I asked Dad what time it was, and he took off his wristwatch and handed it to me. He told me the surgery had taken about four hours.

By the time they brought me back to my room from the recovery room, I was becoming more alert and aware. I had a catheter in, which was very uncomfortable, but at least it would be coming out pretty soon.

I had staples for sutures down my neck where they had opened me up to get at my cervical spine. The incision started at the very top of my neck, just below where the bottom of my skull meets my neck, and extended down to a little bit below my shoulder blades. Apparently, they wanted to visually inspect my entire cervical spine.

Just below the small of my back, on the left side, where they sawed bone off the pelvic crest, it was very sore, just as the doctors said it would be. I had an upside-down smiley face incision there that had been sutured.

But considering they had drilled holes through two of my cervical vertebrae and ran wire through those holes – not to mention they opened me up like a quartered chicken breast – I suppose the pain I was feeling was acceptable. As a matter of fact, so long as they had me pumped full of morphine, just about anything was acceptable.

Dr. Joyce met with me on the day after the operation, on Saturday, and said that everything went well with the surgery. He said I'd get a new neck brace on Monday, and if everything continued to go well, we'd also talk on Monday about getting me discharged sometime next week.

On Monday, the doc sent me to radiology for more X-rays of my neck. When he got them, he read them and said everything looked good. He sent me to the brace clinic to get the kind of brace I would wear for the rest of my recovery time, which would be roughly ten weeks.

They fitted me for a Philadelphia collar – a plastic, two-piece brace that was adjustable by fastening a Velcro strap on either side.

The brace had a little indent inside the front where my chin could rest, and the back of it went up to the middle of the back of my head.

It was sturdy but it was lightweight, and it was comfortable, especially when compared to some of the metal clunkers I had to wear.

It was easy to adjust and easy to take off, and to put on. So, I was quite happy with the doctor's decision to use the Philadelphia collar. I was also happy with his decision to discharge me on Wednesday morning.

Dr. Joyce came by my bed Wednesday morning at 9 am. He had a slew of papers for me to sign and bring home. Some were about the discharge. Some were about how to take care of a surgically repaired neck; others were about the medications I'd be on.

The medications he was sending me home with were 10 mg. Valium, once daily for muscle spasms; 50 mg. Demerol, twice daily for pain; and 30 mg. codeine, twice daily, for pain.

I was eager to be going home, and I'd gotten dressed in street clothes. My wife and my mother-in-law were coming to pick me up.

It was October 21st, and I hadn't been home since the early morning of Columbus Day, almost two full weeks ago. It had been one hell of a near-fortnight.

I was looking forward to getting home and resuming my life, at least as much as possible. Obviously, I wouldn't be able to work for some time – the doctors were saying three months. It also messed me up in a career sense, too. I had been working for Leon just to earn some money while I was waiting to begin a job at General Electric in Lynn.

My Uncle Bill and my Gramma Doris had both worked at GE for their entire working lives. They wanted to get me in there when I was first out of high school, but I wasn't interested at the time.

At the age of 26, however, I felt differently about it and asked my Uncle Bill if he could still get me in there. He said he could but that, unlike in the past, it would take some time. I told him that I appreciated whatever he could do.

After looking into it, Billy said he could get me in, but it would take about eight months. It was February 1981, and Billy said when a guy there retired, around the end of October, I could replace him. I was thrilled at such an opportunity.

So, 1981 was a countdown to when I'd be able to start at General Electric River Works in Lynn. The target date worked out to be in late October or early November.

Unfortunately for me, I fractured my cervical spine just a few weeks ahead of when I would have started there. My golden opportunity was tragically shot all to hell.

What would carry me forward, even if it didn't directly put any dollars or food on the table, was my composing.

It would be maybe three months before I could resume drumming in my band. My bandmates had assured me that my job with the band was secure.

They said they might use a substitute drummer to play a few gigs, but once I was able to resume my place on the drums, it was definitely my domain.

This was, frankly, a big deal to me and helped keep my spirit afloat during this arduous and testing time. The accident had cost me so much. It mattered a lot to me that my job as the drummer in the Marginals and in the Blue Chips was secure.

My bandmates – my fellow Musketeers – were loyal, through and through. Their loyalty meant a lot to me. It's not an abundant commodity in this life.

I had been in the middle of composing a large orchestral work for a concert band when I had the car wreck.

I had met with Maestro John Corley, conductor of the Massachusetts Institute of Technology concert band, earlier in the year when the piece was in its early stages. He'd been very enthusiastic about the composition, and because of his interest, I tailored the work for the concert band.

Our hope was that it could eventually be performed by the MIT concert band, with Mr. Corley conducting, at one of their future programs.

To continue working on the composition, I found it necessary to tack the 32-stave manuscript pages up on the wall.

I couldn't, for example, sit at a table and look down at sheet music or at anything else because I couldn't move my neck.

Being immobilized in the neck brace meant that I couldn't look down. The solution for me to be able to continue writing music was to tack the pages up on my wall. This way, I could read and write on the pages just by looking straight ahead.

When I was writing my first symphony, I employed the same method. I did it not because of any mobility problem but because I found it easier to realize and feel the flow of the composition if I could read it from beginning to end, along the wall, rather than turning pages, one page at a time.

This time, I was using the vertical alignment out of necessity. I simply couldn't work at a desk or a table. It was the best alternative and an easy choice, given that it was a method of composing I had experience with.

Working on the composition fell into a nighttime routine. With my wife Nan at home and our two-year-old son toddling about, the best time for me to compose was at night.

Once little Phil and Nan were in bed, I could get to work. Ordinarily, they went to bed around eight o'clock.

I had two pianos in the music room, which was also the den. I had a turn-of-the-century, grand, upright piano, built around 1900, and a spinet piano from a Newton Centre club that had discarded it. I did all of my composing and most of my playing on the upright, which had a rich tone and excellent clarity in the lower range.

With the house quiet and no interruptions, work on the composition proceeded at a brisk pace. It was around 11 pm each night that I noticed just how high I was on the painkillers. Enhanced by the Valium, the Demerol and codeine had me dieseled. I was junked up and feeling no pain. Still, the work continued at a good clip.

The composition 'A Very Impressionable Age,' I had originally composed for solo jazz piano. But now, adapting it for a concert band, I was excited about the orchestrations I could build using the instruments of a concert band. I had an affinity for the work as it was written for solo piano, but getting the chance to present it using the instrumentation of a concert band was a rare opportunity. It opened up possibilities of pure aural delight.

It was an intelligent, cerebral work, and the finished product was going to sound really great.

Night after night, my routine didn't change, and the only difference from one night to the next was when I finished and went to bed. Mostly, I'd call it a night between 1 and 3 o'clock.

I was committed to producing an exciting, professional, and polished composition for MIT to perform.

After four weeks, my neck felt like it was healing and doing better. I was able to work on a flat surface again and worked at the kitchen table, which made the work of notation faster and far less tricky than working on a vertical page tacked up on the wall.

I was finishing up a long night of writing when, around 3:45 am, I suddenly experienced burning hot pain in my neck, and my ears started ringing. It was like a fire alarm going off when there really was a fire. It was frightening and demanded my immediate, undivided attention.

I stopped what I was doing and made sure to sit in a very straight and erect position. I had to figure out what was safe to do next. The sudden pain and ringing in my ears signaled that something bad had happened or was happening. I was going to have to get myself to the hospital.

It was almost four am, and the busses started running after 5 am, in about an hour. I didn't have the cash to pay for a cab, so I'd have to take a bus to the train station and a train into Boston to the Mass General Hospital.

I didn't know exactly what was going on in my surgically repaired c-spine, but whatever it was, it wasn't good.

Taking the subway into Boston, I had plenty of time to speculate what might have happened to my neck. One possibility that I dreaded was that my neck had become unstable and would need to be immobilized in a Halo brace. I was bummed out at the prospect of being hospitalized in a Halo brace.

It wasn't an unlikely next step, but there were also many other possibilities. I'd simply have to wait and see what the surgeon had to say about it.

I arrived at the emergency room, and Dr. Joyce was summoned. He examined me, asked a lot of questions, and then sent me for X-rays.

After the X-rays had been taken and forwarded to Dr. Joyce, he called me into his office, where he had several of the X-rays up on a lighted wall, where he could read them.

He called me over to the X-rays to show me what he had discovered. First, he had two X-rays displayed, one on top of the other. The X-ray on the bottom was one they'd just taken, and on top was an X-ray of the same area that had been taken right after my surgery, a little over a month ago.

It was the area of C-7, where he had drilled a small, round hole through C-7 itself and ran #18 gauge stainless-steel wire through it.

In the old X-ray, I could clearly see the small circular hole they had drilled in C-7, but in the current X-ray, that hole was markedly elongated. Rather than a round hole, it now looked slot-shaped or oval.

Because my neck was not immobilized enough and was moving, even if not all that much, that movement was causing the wire to rip through the bone of my vertebrae. As a result, the round hole in C-7 had become an elongated, slot-shaped hole.

Sooner or later, the wire would tear all the way through C-7. Once that happened, my neck would be as unstable as when I first broke it, if not worse.

The bottom line was if my cervical spine was fractured and moving around, not only would it not heal, but it could adversely impact my spinal cord. I could become paralyzed.

Dr. Joyce showed me how the wire was ripping through my vertebrae and said the only solution was to put me in a Halo brace. He said a Halo brace was the only way to completely immobilize my neck, and to be sure that it would heal properly.

I tried to avoid it. I promised I'd stay in bed and not move my neck for as long as was necessary. But even as I heard myself saying it, I knew it wasn't possible. It was my fear of talking. I didn't want to be hospitalized, and I didn't want my head screwed to a hospital bed headboard.

My misconceptions about Halo braces would soon be coming to an end.

Dr. Joyce said there was no other approach; a Halo brace was required to get me back on track.

God damned, Leon and his baloney skin tires were the cause of all this. And that son of a bitch wanted me to pay him 400 dollars to cover the deductible on his auto insurance. What a weasel.

Within the bad news, however, there was also some good news. I didn't have to be hospitalized in order to wear a Halo brace.

I had an image of an old John Wayne movie in mind, where the patient has a broken neck, and his head is screwed into a round, Halo-like rim, which is set into the headboard of his hospital bed.

Looking back, no wonder I was fearful of a Halo brace. The thought of one's head being screwed to the headboard of a bed is enough to fill any sane man with terror.

Dr. Joyce and another doctor assisting him were going to put me into a Halo brace. For the occasion, they had moved me to a small hospital room, where I was sitting in a chair, wondering what was going to happen next.

The doctors had all kinds of stainless-steel parts and hardware scattered around them. They had two large toolboxes full of Allen wrenches, crescent wrenches, sockets, plyers, screwdrivers, and the like. The toolboxes could have belonged to an auto mechanic.

Dr. Joyce gave me a quick overview of the procedure. They would attach a metal rim to my head. They would also fit me to wear a Halo vest that looked like a flak jacket, and finally, four metal rods would connect the metal rim around my head to the Halo vest on my chest.

Once installed, there'd be no movement possible in my neck, which was the idea.

If I wanted to look left or right, I'd have to turn left or right at the waist to do it. The same applied to looking up or down; I'd have to bend forward at the waist to look down or bend backward to look up.

They said that because of the restrictions, the Halo brace imposed, my peripheral vision would sharply improve.

The first thing they did was mark four spots on my skull where the Halo rim would be anchored.

There was no general anesthesia or an operating table. Instead, they had me sitting in a plain chair that you might find in a cafeteria.

They made their four marks, the front two just forward of my temples on either side and the rear two they put a half-inch behind my ears, about even with the top of my ears.

They held the Halo temporarily in place with little suction cups that stuck to my skull while they very carefully marked the spots where they would anchor the Halo rim.

Next, they injected my skin and scalp at each mark with a numbing agent, using a syringe that was the size of a diabetic's needle.

They waited fifteen or twenty minutes for the numbing agent to take full effect, then resumed numbing my skull at the same four points, this time using a large syringe with a large needle.

At each point, the needle made a crunching sound as they pushed it far enough into my skull to totally numb the areas where they would drive in the screws or pins that anchor the Halo rim in place.

They did one spot at a time, and when they had all four done, we again waited for the numbing agent to take full effect.

Next, Dr. Joyce sank the screws that anchored the Halo very firmly into my skull. I was a bit surprised when I saw them using a torque wrench to put the screws in. It was the exact same wrench that I'd seen auto mechanics using many times.

Apparently, they use it so they know the exact pressure they're exerting when they're sinking the pins into the skull.

Sinking the pins caused an even larger, louder bone-crunching sound than the hypodermic needles had made earlier.

The pins were 3/8" in diameter and had a pointed or beveled tip to them. With the pins, there was a lot more stainless steel pushing through bone than there had been with the hypodermic needles, and the crunching sound increased accordingly.

But for all the sound effects of crunching bone, I didn't feel any pain from it. The only discomfort I experienced was pressure building in my head. The further along they got, sinking the four pins, the greater the pressure I felt in my head.

At one point, I said to the doctors that it felt like my head was going to bust open like a watermelon dropped onto the sidewalk. They said not to worry, it was normal and that the sensation would subside and go away shortly.

With the Halo securely anchored in place, they helped me into the Halo vest that I'd be wearing for the next few months.

There was a lot of stainless-steel hardware attached to either side of the Halo that, in turn, held the rods that ran from the Halo down to the flak vest.

Four stainless-steel rods are attached to the hardware on either side of the Halo, two on the left side, front and back, and two on the right side, front and back.

The other ends of the rods were then attached to the flak vest on the left side and right side, front and back, at chest level.

The doctors checked their work, first going over the hardware and its nuts and bolts. They rechecked the Halo and the pins holding it in place and went over the Halo vest.

Lastly, they checked with me on how my supply of painkillers was holding up.

Before I agreed to undergo the Halo procedure, Dr. Joyce had promised me carte blanche as far as painkillers were concerned. Now, he was making good on that promise.

After they finished installing the Halo brace, he suggested Percocet for me to go with the codeine and Valium, but I told him I'd rather remain on Demerol. I said that together with the codeine and Valium, the Demerol had worked very well in controlling the pain and the muscle spasms as well.

Looking back at it, my choice of pain pills surprises me a bit, but it really doesn't matter. With the injury I had, the need for pain pills was legitimate and necessary. The problem with the whole thing for me, no matter which pain pills I chose, was that I carried the disease of addiction.

I didn't look at the situation from a pain management perspective. For me, it was an opportunity to get high. I was practically giddy with the anticipation of getting high. It wasn't a rational choice; it's simply how I'm wired.

I wasn't ready to handle these drugs. I didn't have the skills to prevent the high-speed train wreck that, sooner or later, was going to be me. It was heading my way, and I wasn't even aware of it.

I had come to the hospital by subway, but now that I was wearing a Halo brace, Dr. Joyce wanted me to take a taxicab home to Malden. He didn't want me negotiating the subways and busses, having just been newly fitted with a Halo brace.

Dr. Joyce arranged the cab ride home for me, but first, I had to stop off at the MGH pharmacy with new prescriptions. Once the scripts were filled, I was ready to go back home.

The cab picked me up at the front entrance on Fruit Street. I couldn't help but wonder what I must have looked like to the cab driver. Something exotic or weird? I also couldn't help wondering how the screws, they called pins, were going to feel in my skull once the numbing agent wore off.

The rods that went from the Halo vest and connected to the Halo rim were quite long and extended above the Halo rim by a foot. This meant they also extended above the top of my head by about six inches.

Also, the rods were placed at an angle in such a way that, as they ran from my vest up to the Halo rim, they veered away from me and out to the sides.

The result was that my clearance didn't depend on my head and shoulders but rather depended on the four rods. Those rods extended out in front of me, behind me, and out to the sides of me. Which meant I had to be very careful, for example, when walking through doorways.

It also meant that if I tried to lie on my back, I wouldn't be able to. The two rods in the back would reach the bed first, and my back and shoulders would be suspended about six inches above the bed.

The same was true if I wanted to sleep on my side. The two rods, front and back, left side or right side, would meet the bed surface before my side did.

Being unable to lie down so that my shoulders and back were actually in contact with the bed was annoying. Being suspended above the bed was an uncomfortable and rather creepy feeling that took time to adjust to.

The best solution, according to the Halo brace owner's manual handbook, was to sleep sitting up at an angle, like in a recliner. So, after discussing it with my family, it was decided that the best approach was to rent a powered hospital bed that could raise and lower the head and foot of the bed.

To that end, my mom and my Gramma Doris drove to my house that afternoon so we could search for a place to rent a bed.

We easily found a Medford pharmacy that rented hospital equipment of all types, and they rented a hospital bed to us, which they delivered and installed that same afternoon.

At first, I wasn't getting much sleep, but after a few weeks, I began sleeping better. Lying propped up by the Halo rods above the surface of the bed really creeped me out in the beginning.

Whether I lay on my back or on my side, I was suspended above the surface of the bed. Being suspended that way, it felt as if gravity was pulling me down and was going to pull my head right out of the Halo rim.

Rational or not, during the first couple of weeks, it was an uncomfortable way to sleep. The thought of the screws being ripped out by the pull of gravity was none too comfortable either.

Sleep wasn't very easy to come by. But as time went by, I finally got more accustomed to the awkward and uncomfortable facts of wearing a Halo brace.

I got to where I could sleep on my back and even on my side, albeit elevated above the bed by the rods. At long last, I was learning to sleep in what had been the most difficult and unpleasant of reclining positions.

Work on my composition had greatly slowed down. Wearing the Halo brace was just too awkward and distracting. It impeded my capacity to think clearly and broadly enough to compose for a large group of instruments like a concert band. Work continued, but at a much-reduced rate of what I had been doing prior to the Halo brace.

In the early going, I had a couple of mishaps with my Halo brace.

One morning when the telephone rang, I was sitting at the kitchen table right next to the wall phone, so I answered it.

Forgetting that I was wearing a Halo brace, I firmly clamped the receiver to my right ear. Unfortunately, before the receiver reached my ear, it clanged off the Halo rim and rod.

Slamming the Halo with the telephone receiver caused a strong ringing in the Halo and in the rods on that side. The ringing or vibration focused at the right-front screw, or pin, and moved through my skull and into my head.

The reverberation wasn't as painful as an ice cream headache, but the buzzing along the Halo and into my head was very uncomfortable and a bit painful. It was definitely not to be repeated, and I remained careful with the telephone thereafter.

A week later, I was walking from the kitchen into the living room. The doorway to the living room was rather narrow, and I badly misjudged it as I was going through. I banged the right-front Halo rod hard off the side of that doorway.

The result was that I nearly tore the right-front pin entirely out of my skull. As it was, that pin got banged hard, and although it did spring back to its original position, getting moved around violently made the screw hole larger.

The pin became loose from being moved around and started oozing a little bit of clear, sticky fluid.

From when it happened in the morning until the end of the day, I had to dry the area around that screw hole three or four times.

Over the next couple of days, I followed the same routine, cleaning the area with a Q-tip a couple of times.

By the third day, the discharge stopped, and the screw hole stayed dry. The pin seemed stable and solid after that, and there were no further problems with it.

I was very lucky that I didn't 'pop' a screw. Patients wearing Halos sometimes pop a screw or two or more screws.

It doesn't necessarily happen from banging the Halo brace, it can happen for no apparent reason while sitting quietly in a chair.

I don't know what causes it, but some people pop one or more of their screws, while others never do.

I saw a fellow patient who had popped a screw sitting on a gurney in the waiting room of the MGH outpatient brace clinic. The guy was wearing a Johnny and had come in by ambulance from a rehabilitation hospital. This meant that, most likely, he'd been paralyzed to some extent.

His doctor was going to set a replacement pin for the one that had popped out. When they replace a pin, they have to set the pin in a new area. The old spot is not viable and cannot be used.

Initially, I was taken aback that his doctor, with a torque wrench in hand, was going to reset the pin in the waiting room. I thought the privacy of a triage room was the more appropriate place.

Nonetheless, his doc started torquing the man's pin, asking again and again if he was alright. He constantly wanted to know how his patient was feeling, and I knew why. He was putting in the replacement pin without having numbed the man's skull.

The doctor continued torquing and asking, but at one point, the guy simply passed out and fell back onto the gurney where he'd been sitting.

As I looked around at the other patients in the waiting room, I realized that most of them were on gurneys and had come for maintenance from rehab hospitals. I was probably the only patient there who wasn't a paraplegic or quadriplegic.

Every Saturday morning, my father drove me to the Mass General Hospital for my weekly Halo brace maintenance appointment.

He arrived each Saturday morning at 7:30, and we drove over to the MGH brace clinic, where they went over my Halo with a fine-tooth comb.

Mostly, they tightened all the nuts and bolts associated with the Halo's hardware and rods. They also checked the connections where the rods went from the Halo rim to the flak vest.

For the grand finale, they'd tighten the pins that were sunk into my skull.

The first week that Dad and I went into the brace clinic was Dad's first time being around the maintenance routine. He wasn't ready for the clearly audible sound of crunching bone that occurred whenever they torqued the Halo rim pins into my skull.

Poor dad bolted out of the room to get out of earshot of the gruesome sound. It was my first experience undergoing the tune-up, too, but I had heard the crunching bone sound before when they first installed the Halo. It does make an impression.

Dad told me later that he was grossed out by the crunch, crunch sound of my skull being bored into.

Dad was very supportive from the beginning, starting when he kept watch at my bedside in the recovery room after surgery. He brought me into my Saturday morning appointments at MGH every week, from beginning to end.

I had lost the opportunity to begin working at GE in Lynn because of the broken neck, and I wasn't working for Leon anymore. On top of that, because Leon had paid me as a contractor instead of as an employee, I couldn't collect the unemployment benefits to which I should have been entitled. All in all, financially, I was in bad shape.

I had all the usual bills to pay, like rent, electric, phone, cable, and now that it was heating season, it cost a couple hundred dollars every time the oil tank needed filling.

The problem was I had no paycheck coming in and no savings to draw from. I had no assets to speak of that I could sell to raise funds.

Our families would be able to help a little bit, but the fact of the matter was I had bills coming due and no way to pay them.

Leon only had the minimum allowable auto insurance on his VW, but if I had anything at all coming, I certainly needed it.

I called his insurance company several times, trying to get a clear picture of what compensation, if any, I might be eligible for. It took several weeks, but eventually, I received $2,000. PIP check in the mail from the insurance company.

The money didn't just come in handy; it saved my ass and got me into the new year with my head financially above water. In the long term, however, I had a lot of unanswered questions.

The question about how I'd make a living would have to wait until I had an answer to the other question, which was, 'How able-bodied will I be when I'm fully healed?'

It had been five weeks since I had the Halo brace put on and nine weeks since I had the cervical fusion. I had been in one kind of neck brace or another for ten weeks, but the Halo brace was the worst of it.

Dec. 19, after my usual Saturday morning appointment at the MGH brace clinic, they told me to come back the next Thursday to possibly get the Halo brace removed.

The next week, on Christmas Eve day, I showed up for my appointment with bells on. They took some X-rays, compared them with even more X-rays, and then finally removed the Halo brace.

When they backed out the pins, I had a very odd sensation. Just as the insertion of the pins created a feeling of pressure in my head, their removal triggered the release of that pressure. What made it strange was that I hadn't been feeling the pressure anymore, but it must have been there all along because when the pins came out, I could feel the pressure being released.

Suddenly, I had that pressure again, and then, in a flash, it was gone.

It was a beautiful, early Christmas present having that Halo brace removed. I was finally out of the flak vest, out of the Halo rim, and the rest of it. No more rods, no more screws and pins, and no more crunching bone. I was free.

The Halo brace handbook stated that wearing a Halo would not persuade the wearer to associate it with Halo's and angels. It said, in fact, the wearer might even associate it with the other end of that spectrum, as in devils and demons.

I wouldn't disagree with the Halo handbook's sentiment because it is a rugged, punishing contraption, but it did enable my broken neck to heal properly.

By March 1982, I had started rehearsing again with my band, The Marginals. It felt good to be drumming again. Physically, my neck handled it fine, and psychologically. It was a big step towards living a normal life again.

In April I was offered the opportunity to work on inground swimming pools, a business that I was familiar with.

The offer came from a man I knew when I had been in the business. He had been something of a competitor when I was selling and installing both above-ground and inground swimming pools.

Since I didn't have a pool company anymore, I had no problem taking the man up on his offer to have me put in some of his pools. I could certainly use the money.

The first job was finishing a cement wall inground pool that was about half done. It turned out that putting in the stairs, shaping the bottom, and dropping a liner – all normal steps for this type of pool – was putting too much strain, too much force on my newly repaired broken neck.

Even carrying a roll of black polypipe was too much. I was healed but not ready for swimming pool construction work.

With the benefit of hindsight, I can say that I would have been fine doing that kind of work if I had waited four or five more years. But in 1982, just six months following surgery and three months since the Halo brace had come off, it was just too soon to tax my neck to that extent.

Drumming was one thing, but humping around a construction site was quite another thing.

I was disappointed about not being able to work on the pools, to be sure, but things with the band were going well, and that meant I was batting .500.

Following my failed attempt to return to swimming pool construction, I was still trying to think of some way that I could earn a full-time living. To that end, I went to the employment office in Malden Square later that same month of April.

I was hoping maybe they could get me started with some kind of a job. But it seemed as soon as I brought up the subject of finding work, the clerk brought up the subject of not being able to help me.

I was frustrated, and I blurted out to the clerk something like, 'What does a person do when he's been injured and can no longer perform the kind of work he's done in the past?'

Before the clerk could say anything, somebody in line behind me said, "Go to Mass Rehab!"

He was referring to the Massachusetts Rehabilitation Commission, about which I knew absolutely nothing. But in the coming months, I would become well-acquainted with it.

I called up Mass Rehab and made an appointment to be seen. The first thing they did was ask me what I wanted to get out of their program. It was a basic screening.

I explained about being physically unable to do the pool

construction work that I used to do. I went through the story about working on a pool job in April and simply not being up to it.

I went over the injury I sustained back in October 1981. I also filled out several forms, which took up most of the two hours I was there on that first visit.

At my next appointment two weeks later, I was assigned to a counselor named Nathan Zoll. Mr. Zoll talked to me about the kinds of programs they had at Mass Rehab. He also asked me about what kind of career I might be interested in.

I told him I was interested in working as a computer programmer, and he seemed to go along with the idea. But first, I would have to prove that I could do that kind of work. To that end, he had me take some tests that were geared to measuring intelligence and aptitude.

When I came in next time he had my test results, and I had scored well enough to get approved and funded for studying computer programming.

Over the next few weeks, we put together a proposal for me to attend the computer school, Control Data Institute. Control Data Institute was in Woburn and was operated by the big mainframe builder, Control Data Corporation.

To get certified, I'd have to finish a 980-hour computer programming and operations curriculum and pass all the tests.

At the end of the 980-hour program, they'd administer a final test, having me write several computer programs in four different programming languages: Basic, COBOL, Fortran, and RPGII.

I was confident I could do the work, and Mr. Zoll was confident that I could, too.

He submitted a vocational rehabilitation proposal for me, and by the end of July, it was approved with full funding. It was beginning to look like it really was going to happen.

Mr. Nathan Zoll really carried the ball for me at Mass Rehab. But once school started, I'd be the one carrying that ball, and it was an exciting prospect. I was scheduled to begin at Control Data Institute in four months, in December.

I had broken my neck the previous October in 1981. It was nine months later, and I was still taking the same dosages of the same pain-killing meds I was given when I first came home from the hospital.

I simply continued taking the meds without any plan for managing them, such as slowly cutting down over time and eventually stopping. Why would I want to stop? They made me feel good, and I liked feeling good. That's as far as my addict's thinking went on the subject back then.

The doctors didn't seem to mind, and they never had anything negative or critical to say on the subject whenever I called up for another set of refills. It was like they were giving me permission by default. So, everything seemed okay.

By the fall, though, nearly a year after the accident, I started to feel differently about it. I had the rock band going, I was composing a piece for the MIT concert band, and I was starting computer programming school soon. I needed to have all my wits about me.

I called up the Mass General and told them I wanted to come in to discuss changing my medications. As a matter of fact, I wanted to stop taking the Demerol and the codeine all together.

I was told to come in, and we could talk about it. When I got to the hospital, it turned out that because it was a Saturday, the doctors on duty weren't the ones who were familiar with my case. They wouldn't be in until Monday, so the doctor on duty who was tending to me simply wrote out fresh prescriptions for my current meds and sent me on my way with an appointment for Monday morning.

When I arrived at the hospital on Monday and looked at my appointment card, I saw for the first time that my appointment had been scheduled with Acute Psychiatric Services or the APS department.

On Saturday, and again today, addressing my desire to come off the meds, was proving to be more difficult than I thought it would be.

When I was called into the doctor's office for my appointment,

I got a big surprise. The doctor handed me a small sheet of paper with the name, address and appointment date of my referral.

When I asked him what it was that he was referring me to, he said, "It's a methadone clinic. You can start there in two weeks."

I was surprised by the fact that he gave me a referral to a methadone clinic without first having a discussion with me about it. In fact, he didn't say much of anything to me.

Perhaps he had looked through my history and seen prior experiences with addiction that had been overcome with methadone detox. Although those had been addictions to heroin, not at all resembling the pain med addiction I now face, I can understand the thinking that if methadone worked several times before, it should be tried again.

Still, I would have felt better about it if the doctor had spoken with me about it rather than informing me in a rather perfunctory fashion.

At any rate, I was taken by surprise at this unexpected outcome. But it didn't take me long to embrace the idea of going onto a methadone program.

It was the beginning of November 1982 when I started at the Tufts Methadone Clinic. It was located in the Boston theatre district, and it was a very short-term program of six months duration, max.

I had wanted to stay on methadone for longer than six months, but six months was it at Tufts. So, I put my name in the Boston City

Hospital Methadone Program, which was a 2-year program. I hoped I could transfer there before my six months at Tufts was up.

The Tufts program was kind of a stripped-down program. The max stay there was 6 months, and I don't remember being assigned to a counselor or having to go to group meetings.

It didn't take too long before I was totally off the Demerol and codeine and stabilized on a dosage of methadone. At thirty milligrams, the methadone did all of the work that the Demerol and codeine had been doing and then some. The truth is, in the first weeks on methadone, it gave me a pleasant buzz.

For better or worse, I was all in at the Tufts clinic.

In late November, I decided to change my start date at Control Data Institute from December '82 to March 1983.

I didn't feel ready to start at CDI. The little bit of preparation I had been doing with the study material left me feeling terribly inadequate. It was all too much of a mystery to me.

I hoped that by the time I began in March, I'd feel a bit more comfortable and at home with the material.

As it turned out, deferring my start at CDI proved to be a good move. The extra three months to get to know the material better was well worth it.

Back in December, I didn't have a clue. But with the additional time, I got past the culture shock of learning about computers and programming them. Now that I was familiar with the concepts and the material, I felt ready to give it a shot.

Things went well for me at Control Data Institute. Working through the curriculum, we studied and proceeded at our own pace. I liked it that way, and when I had questions, I could ask an instructor or a fellow student.

By the end of July, I was ready to start on the three COBOL programs I had to write. It was one of the final elements I had to complete to graduate.

Some of the students had given nicknames to those programs. I remember they called the last one "The Bear" because it was large and difficult.

I had finished the first two COBOL programs without trouble, but it seemed the students were right about the third one. It was a bear, and adding to the difficulty was the sheer length of it.

In an effort to understand and solve the problems I had run into on COBOL program #3, I asked a student who had already finished that program if I could look over his solution. He was fine with letting me have a gander at it.

A little while back, I had recorded some music for him onto a couple of cassette tapes, and he was glad for the chance to return the favor.

After studying his solution to the program, it was fairly easy for me to write one of my own. By the beginning of September, I had turned it in for grading, completing the final exercise of the 980-hour curriculum.

All that was left for me to do was to assemble job search information for the vocational department at Control Data Institute. Beyond that, there remained only the task of landing an entry-level programming job and, thus, launching a career.

The Control Data Institute vocational counselors had seemed very upbeat and positive whenever we discussed starting a career in computer programming.

I had finished the course ahead of schedule and had nothing left to do study-wise. The only school-related thing that remained was graduation.

Graduation was in October, and technically, it was at graduation when I'd be officially certified in computer programming and operations. Until then, I was just marking time, but I didn't mind. I'd been putting in long hours of study for six months, and I welcomed the chance to pause and take a breath.

October 1983 graduation was fast approaching at CDI, but a week before it, I got a big surprise. A Boston-based direct mail marketing company, Hub Mail Advertising, wanted to hire me.

The pay wasn't great, but it was respectable for an entry-level position. After a year, I'd become eligible for health benefits and savings plans.

I never had a salaried job before. I had always worked by the hour or been paid by the job as a contractor. So, this was a first for me.

There was something about being offered a job that paid a salary that said I was a professional.

Granted, my self-esteem was a bit inflated by this good fortune, but after all, I had earned it in more ways than one. You might even say I broke my neck for this job.

The Bob Dole I Knew

Bob Dole was a big man with gruff mannerisms and a gravelly smoker's voice. He was an alcoholic drinker who had survived two house fires of his own making.

My parents rented the first floor of a two-family house from Bob Dole in 1955. The house was located on Superior Street in East Lynn, near the Swampscott line, a short walk from Kings Beach.

We moved there from Burrill St., Swampscott, when I was six months old. Dole, his wife Irene, and their young son lived on the second floor.

When we moved out four years later, my grandmother and uncle moved into the apartment, taking our place. As a result, our frequent visits to Grandma's allowed me to continue seeing my friends on Superior Street throughout the 60's.

When I lived there as a young boy, I had been afraid of Mr. Dole, and I dreaded his presence. He clearly enjoyed picking on me. It seemed that he was always angry, but I also recall him deriving what appeared to be enjoyment from teasing me.

Whenever I saw Dole coming my way, my adrenaline level spiked, and I became full of dread. His manner was brusque, and he was always messing with me. On those occasions, I wanted to disappear and wished my father were there to protect me.

When I was four and five years old, I had a lot of difficulty breathing through my nose because of a deviated septum. This forced me to breathe through my mouth, and it was this habit of mine that became one of Dole's favorite avenues of humiliation.

Dole would confront me to say, "What are you doing with your mouth open? You trying to catch flies in there?" It was one of his preferred taunts.

If Dole's words alone weren't mean enough, his attitude and how he delivered those words more than made up for it. To complete his nemesis checklist, he smelled bad, something like stale sweat, and his breath was hot and sour.

By 1964, Bob Dole was living alone in the top-floor apartment of his two-family house. He had purchased it when he was married and working steadily driving an oil delivery truck.

Since those salad days, Dole's only child had passed away from a terminal disease he had been born with. He'd gotten divorced after his wife Irene left him, and he'd fallen badly to his alcoholism.

There was a big turnout for Thanksgiving dinner at my grandmother's place in Lynn one year. It was 1965, and the house was buzzing with the cheerful chatter of family and good friends.

Everyone sampled hors d'oeuvres, caught up on family news, watched football on TV, and waited to be called to the table for

Grammy Doris' immense feedbag. There were so many of us we broke into three groups seated at three tables.

A little while before sitting down to turkey and ham dinner, there was a knock at the front door of the apartment. Being nearest the door, I answered it. It was the landlord, Bob Dole, from upstairs, and he was shit-faced drunk.

He wore a Pork Pie hat, a pair of socks, and not one stitch more than that. Dole was utterly bare-assed, and he just stood there naked without saying a word.

I also just stood there, not saying anything, while looking back to the adults and waiting for someone to make the next move.

Dick Canfield, a good family friend, came over to the door just as some of the others in the room were beginning to take notice of the weird spectacle.

I came away from the door to let the adults handle the unexpected and undressed guest.

Without resistance or fanfare, Dole departed, and the door closed. It had happened so fast it was almost as if it hadn't happened at all.

Looking to see how the adults were reacting to Dole's nude visit, I watched my mom for a clue. She appeared calm as she rolled her eyes and then began speaking to her brother, my Uncle Bill. They easily brushed the incident off as my mom went back to readying the dinner tables.

Realizing that no harm had been done, I relaxed and allowed myself to be amused. It was just a kooky move by a guy whose brain was pickled in alcohol. I don't think many of the holiday diners were even aware of Dole's 'visit.'

The power Bob Dole once held over me was now gone. He'd been revealed, and on top of that, I was no longer 5 years old. Sadly, he was now just a mild joke, and his behavior brought humiliation only to himself.

His stern, commanding eyes were now watery and unseeing, empty windows to a soul gone dark. The alcoholism and the overload of crushing defeats and disappointments had truly brought him down.

The years that my grandmother lived underneath Bob Dole in the 1960s proved to be solitary and lost years for him.

Alone except for his bottle, the odds should have dictated that he had suffered his full measure of bad breaks, but the odds don't always add up.

Dole fell prey to several more escapades that underscored, in farcical terms, just how deeply and dangerously his life had collapsed. Whether or not Dole even noticed, is an open question.

The next summer, his upstairs apartment was broken into as he slept. The men who broke in found him passed out on the booze and dead to the world. They proceeded to take full advantage of their illicitly gained position.

After plundering all they could of Bob Dole's available belongings, they decided to stay and treat themselves to a home cooked meal.

They took a chicken out of Dole's refrigerator, and cooked it in his oven. They actually had mashed potatoes and vegetables to go with it, which they ate at Dole's kitchen table.

My Uncle Bill appeared mildly amused as he told me the story, and I was amused, too. But I couldn't help but think it was a liability for my Grammy Doris and uncle to live under such goings-on.

Dole's alcoholic adventures weren't always lighthearted and amusing and didn't always result in harmless, anecdotal buffoonery.

At the end of the 1960s, as he fell asleep or passed out, Dole dropped a lit cigarette that started a fire. It wasn't the first time he started a fire in the house, but on this occasion the entire house went up in flames. My grandmother, my uncle, and Dole barely got out of the inferno with their lives.

The house was salvageable but required a huge renovation effort and a long time to complete all the work. Rather than an extended stay at a hotel during the renovation, my grandma and uncle decided to opt for new digs.

They moved, renting another house a half-mile up the street and ending the connection to Bob Dole that had started back in 1955. But it was actually during that nude Thanksgiving Day visit a few years earlier that I had last seen him.

I remembered Dole before the booze brought him down, before his young son died, and before he and his wife had gotten divorced. I had to wonder if he hadn't gotten something of a raw deal.

It's hard enough that his son had been born with a deadly handicap and that it would end his life before he reached the age of 12. Yet things were only going to get much worse for Dole.

Despite frequent requests back when I was a kid living there, I was never allowed to play with the Dole's son. I wasn't even allowed to simply go upstairs to meet him. I had simply been told that he was very sick and bedridden and that he couldn't go out.

By the time I was old enough to make my own decisions, the boy was long since dead, and I'd moved far away. Far removed from the immediacy of it all, both in years and geographically speaking, the Doles had faded from my consciousness.

But every once in a while, even in middle age and beyond, the Doles cross my mind, both in remembrances and in the unanswered questions about the boy, the adults, and what they did with their lives.

Perhaps Dole rode me so hard way back then because I reminded him of his son, and his son's condition had broken his heart. On top of that, I surmise that he was freaking angry about the whole damn thing.

Howaya Beta Endorphins?

Sixteen hours into April Fools Day and I'm still holding my breath. I can't recall anything special ever happening to me on April 1st, or anything happening whatsoever on April Fools Day, save for a blizzard in 1997. But I've had a sense this day that I should be careful and deliberate, so I'm being extra cautious.

When I got clean, I determined that I needed to pay more attention to my own instincts and trust them more, so this is good practice.

It's Social Security Day here in Chelsea, so it will be a wild night in this nutty city and in this building, meaning there will be more than an ample need to mind one's business and surroundings. Of course, there is the fact that I stay to myself and in my own digs, which cuts down on the probability of random surprise.

But off-chance horror, hit-and-runs, KO sucker punches, muggings, assaults, hold-ups, knifings, general harassment, the crazies, the many flavors of desperate, the sociopathic, sadistic thrill seekers, the violently inebriated, the gangs, the paranoid crack head, and the unintended stray bullet, the gas explosion, the out-of-control car in a police chase, the falling tree limbs, falling bricks, falling power lines and other urban shrapnel always happen to somebody.

I won't expect the likes of Batman or Spiderman to bail me out; Arnold Schwarzenegger or Harrison Ford will not be saving the day.

Be wary and be responsible about what you do and what you think, lest the lord sees to it that you choke to death while you're eating your steak and cheese sub sandwich. Ignore the rants and ravings of all the paranoid, foolhardy psychos. Take with a large mountain of salt the rambling moralizing of those who hide their insanity behind unusual calm and refinement, and don't fall to the narrow-minded mob mentality that cheapens and diminishes anything and everything.

In the meantime, it has passed into April 2nd with no incidents of note having occurred. Exactly the boring, worry-free 50s that I promised myself I'd have.

Pennies From Purgatory

I put only a penny in the bus fare box. I said "sorry" to the bus driver while making direct eye contact. The driver said very amiably, "It's ok." I thought, 'Think of it as a good penny, not a bad penny.' I'm getting by on the pennies of life.

And no drinking or drugs, no bad behavior, no cutting corners.

Sometimes it's hard, and sometimes I feel crushed, but I manage to feel ok most of the time, within limits. I don't want this life; I don't wish to get too comfortable in the broke and broken ways of living in this shelter.

My SSA checks got suspended due to the felony warrant that was issued for me. It's a felony warrant issued in error. Nonetheless, my landlady put me out until I get the checks reinstated and in my hands, and thus into her hands.

I took steps to do this, first surrendered to the court, then brought confirmation from the court to the Social Security Administration, who says I'll start receiving my checks again in 'about 5 weeks.'

So, until then, I'm back at the Long Island shelter, and I'm waiting.

I'm awaiting the first SSA check, the check that will spring me from here and back to a more normal life, a dollar-ed life, uncollared from this sad environment where I just spent four years of my life, and breaking a lifelong addiction and poverty, to escape this hell, and bringing every fiber of my being to bear in order to achieve it. So, being back here is no easy pill to swallow. My modest life, with at least a few buckeroos to live on, never looked so good. I'm quietly marking time and need to keep this simple and uncomplicated: my spot at the apartment is assured. The passage of about 5 weeks is the only requirement to resuming my life. Think about what I was facing when I first arrived on this island in July of 2000. All the hard work has been done, and if you think about it, you should feel good about what you accomplished, so give yourself a break. The wait is just a couple of Red Sox home stands long.

Wild Dogs and Wild Drugs

I did my part; I passed along the message. It seemed like a win-win situation. One girl needed a phone charger; another one had an extra charger of the same exact model. But when I asked about it, as she was charging her phone with my phone charger, she said, "She wants money for it."

I thought but didn't say, 'what did you think she wants? She wants reasonable compensation.'

It was then that I realized she wasn't at all accustomed to paying for things with cash. In this case, she couldn't simply trade sexual service for what she wanted, as was her customary method of acquiring goods and services.

For her, here in Chelsea, Mass., situations where she has to pay hard cash are rare, and she tries to stay away from them. By her thinking, paying cash for things like a phone charger only wastes the cash she needs for buying crack, heroin, and Klonopin.

The only things she uses cash for seem to be drugs, take-out food, and repaying small cash loans. Purchasing any of the other everyday things with cash only detracts from her ability to buy drugs. Her need for the cash to buy her drugs is a very powerful one, overriding everything else.

The fact is, for many of the things she needs in life, she doesn't need cash on hand or credit. She merely capitalizes on the many local men, and the ones from out of town, who drive through an area called 'the Whore Stroll' who are looking for sex workers or prostitutes. For her, fresh cash is never any further away than a walk up the street.

The easy-fix solution has made her loath to pay with cash for anything except her drugs, and she only makes that concession because dealers won't accept sex for their goods. But the planet will never run dry of men who want what she offers, so she will never run out of dope money for very long.

In Thailand or Indonesia, she might be called the "number one blowjob girl," but this is Chelsea, Massachusetts, in the USA, where she's just another sad victim of addiction, walking the whore stroll.

This environment is not where I would have imagined my new, sober life in recovery might be. But since I am here, I can serve as a good example, or at least as an example of sobriety, and hope.

The abundant drug-abusing behavior around me doesn't deter my mission of staying sober. If it has any effect on me, it's one of affirming the path that I've taken and strengthening it.

But somehow, some way, my addicted friend needs something much more than my example. But setting an example is the best that I can do for her.

Nobody can live someone else's life for them, and no one can get somebody else sober. She'll have to do that herself.

We men are a pack of wild dogs with the never-ending need to have our intimate, sexual selves attended to. It is, I suppose, good news for the sex workers of the world.

The world will never run out of men who need attention, and it won't run short of those offering to provide it for a fee any time soon.

So, she declares, "She wants money for it? Cripes, a new phone with a charger only costs about twelve bucks." I reply, "Right, so how much could she want?"

I knew that she had just spent forty bucks on crack and another forty on heroin, but she still had no cigarettes and was bumming mine.

It reminded me of what my friend, Maz, says about the endless parade of people bumming cigarettes, especially here in Chelsea. She says, "Why don't they short their dealers ten bucks and buy themselves a pack of cigarettes?" She always has terrific sayings to exemplify her solid take on common sense.

But most drug addicts won't spend their cash on anything but dope, which is fine as far as I'm concerned. But they shouldn't expect me to subsidize their other needs, like cigarettes. Unless, of course, this wild dog needs attending.

Bridge Burners

The chief arsonist of the bridge burner's brigade came by looking for a light. Smoking my cigarettes, bumming my money, drinking my soda, and wiping out my short resources with assurance and cool. She's a practiced bridge burner of long-standing, and she is starting to lean on me. She has no doubt used up the goodwill of most of her acquaintances.

When I first knew her, she came close to being banished permanently from coming into my home.

I had to shout and threaten expulsion to get her attention when she imitated a broken record by continually asking me for money for booze and money for crack cocaine.

But the longer I know her, and the more she's around, the less she does it, and the less she whines about her bad fortune, her tough circumstances, and her need for crack and alcohol.

Avoiding those subjects is a good thing, because taking on such dead weight, isn't in the cards for my future, and is not in her future at this address.

I don't wish to be unkind; I had been that as a young man on several occasions, and I regret it. Nevertheless, I won't put up with such baloney, and I don't have enough resources to give them away in blurs of one-way, socially inept transactions.

Maybe the universe is showing me what I need to see, and maybe it's a test, too. Her hanging about is one thing, but her attempts to devour my resources are quite another thing and will have to cease.

Some contributions are required, and that's reasonable, but I see a problem brewing – where she once offered a blowjob periodically, she now seems to be trying to go as long as she can, giving as little sex as she can get away with. But the fact is, I am not going to share my bed with a girl who doesn't want to fuck, ever. I've already been married…

The real question Is, can she stop being a prostitute and a mooch when we're hanging out?

She told me she loved me early in our relationship, which made me think she wasn't right in the head. At the very least, living like she's been living, the norms are most likely confused.

The reality is she shows up when I pick up my prescription medication, and she leaves as soon as it's gone, which is so very transparent and a bit annoying at times.

This past week, she kicked in a little money, and I definitely give her high marks for that, except that maybe that's what got her into the celibate mood.

Perhaps she's feeling she doesn't need to offer me any sex, because she kicked in twenty bucks toward the household, such as it is. But that doesn't cut it.

Even if I'm as mercenary as she, at least in some ways, there's no way I'm going to have a roomie or a relationship with a woman; that's as tit for tat as that.

Still, to be fair, maybe she just wasn't in the mood. I'll have a talk with her about that.

She needs to be putting cash in consistently if she wants to change the nature of our relationship, but I doubt that she's willing to spend much cash money because she needs it for drugs.

The big pink elephant in the rooming house room is that I'm not going to have a relationship with a woman who's an out-of-control addict. I suppose there was a time when I might have, but I'm 53 now, and I've learned a few things about sobriety.

She needs something to replace or to supplement the money she makes on the street. It's a limited game, which is limited by age and opportunity, so it's better if she doesn't depend on prostitution and gets a legitimate income. But that's asking an awful lot, as things stand now.

In the meantime, I'm going to see how much of the girl I can reveal, and once revealed, I'll see what there is beyond her ingesting drugs that can be real, and of substance, and worthwhile.

I can always hook up with bridge burners and prostitutes; a real person, a girlfriend, takes a little more effort.

Missing Jay

I had been listening to Sister Morphine by the Stones and remembering how much my old friend Jay had loved it. He even seemed to somehow identify with it. I guess we all did to a degree.

I've heard the song and the whole album, Sticky Fingers, many times since Jay died in 1973. But since that year, Jay hasn't listened to it even once.

I was thinking that no matter how unlivable his life had become, if he'd just hung on a bit longer, he might have gotten through it. Then again, it's easy for me to say. After all, since I'd known him, Jay was constantly in pain and wishing for an end to the apparent torment that was his existence. He literally longed for an end to his life because he believed it was the only way to end his predicament.

Jay made relatively frequent casual remarks about "ending it all" or other similar statements. I suppose his friends had gotten accustomed to hearing him make such pronouncements because nobody, including myself, ever really said much to him in response. I can remember saying something like, 'Don't say that,' or simply, 'Come on, Jay,' in a tone of admonishment, but I don't think we took him, perhaps, seriously enough.

At first, I was tempted to say that 'he blew it', but it's just too easy for me to second guess him, and it's unfair. I don't want to be harsh or uncharitable in my interpretation. Enough tragedy and sorrow have already transpired, and I don't want to add to it.

I think that because of the disease of addiction, and given the precarious state of his emotional and mental health, things got too deep and too fast for Jay, and they exceeded his ability to cope.

It's so terrible and unspeakably sad. Jay has missed so much and everybody that knew him would be richer for his presence. And perhaps poorer for his absence.

As I listened to 'Sister Morphine' I couldn't help but think how the song was just one thing of the many things that Jay had missed out on.

Remembering that he was barely in his twenties when he died all those many years ago, a shiver passed through me like a cloud shadow moving across a mountain. I felt a tug of regret in my heart.

A fatalist might say his life ran its course. All I know is that from time to time I wish he were here to share an experience, such as listening to the Stones. But of course, there is nothing to be done on that score.

And here I am forty-eight years later, still trying to understand it.

Still Raining

It's raining hard again on this Sunday morning. It rained yesterday, and the day before. Hard rain. Same as all spring long. And the same heavy rain fell last fall, and in the spring before it. Torrential, record-breaking, cats and dogs' stuff. Do you think God, or congress could be persuaded to put the brakes on this record-breaking reign of rain?

I see that Congress is being informed about climatic changes, such as the unusual numbers of hurricanes and tropical storms, rising ocean levels, and the falling temperature of the North Atlantic Gulf Stream, to name a few.

Over forty years ago, in the 1960's, in junior high school, I clearly recall my science teachers often speaking of ecological issues.

They talked about issues such as planetary warming, emissions from cars and factories, the ozone layer sustaining damage, acid rain, plastic refuse overload, but mostly of the greenhouse effect and what we today call our 'carbon footprint.'

Back then, I didn't hear much about global warming outside of science class. The government never said anything about it, that I can recall. Their environmental action was at that time focused on getting people to stop throwing their trash andjunk out onto the streets and highways. Dubbing the refuse as 'litter,' and calling the offenders 'litter bugs,' the campaign carried slogans like, "Don't be a litterbug."

There wasn't as of yet, broad agreement that environmental change for the worse was a reality. Still, in 1970, the Environmental Protection Agency was formed, which led to meaningful regulations on auto and factory emissions being instituted.

Having been born some sixteen years prior to the EPA's inception and subsequent emissions regulations, I can testify to the fact that it's made a difference. I can literally see and smell the change.

Back in the late 1950's I can remember trucks and busses in city traffic leaving enormous, thick clouds of dark gray exhaust from their tailpipes.

Pedestrians either held their breath or breathed in the noxious fumes. Cars left fumes, too. With some cars, it wasn't noticeable, but on others, it was very much in evidence.

Along the streets in urban areas, the smell of carbon monoxide exhaust was strong and simply a way of life. But, once the EPA was founded and protocols were established, things began to change.

The rules on vehicle emissions were tightened; people were restricted or banned from burning leaves; trash pickup began to include recycle bins to separate paper, glass, and plastic, and deposits on soda cans and bottles were instituted.

Granted, these were elemental, almost remedial steps that were taken, but they were much needed, and after all, we had to start somewhere.

The 'Don't be a litterbug' mantra of the federal government had an impact, as did the 'Bottle Bill' here in Massachusetts. The two measures combined to put a big dent in the amount of trash I saw strewn along the roadways, highways and city streets.

When I was a young boy, there seemed to be an awful lot of rusty cans on our streets. When those cans finally got made from materials other than tin, rusty cans disappeared, but the discarded cans remained. It took recycling and deposits to truly get the cans and bottles off the streets.

Beginning in the 1960's and picking up steam into the 1970's, was the concept of health food. People started to seriously address the kinds of food we put into our bodies.

What kind of grain did the hens eat that laid our eggs? Where did they live? In a cage, or on an open range? Are the cattle fed steroids or antibiotics? How does the food break down in terms of cholesterol, fat, protein, and calories? It's all a bit much, and almost nobody has a handle on all of it.

Practically overnight, we became concerned with our environment, with what was in our food, and about where we put in our trash. We became cognizant of what we released into the air. Clean water projects were initiated to clean up polluted rivers and harbors.

The TV and radio commercials incessantly ask, "What's in your laundry soap?" "What's in your paint?" "What's in your body spray?"

In some ways, we have become, in comparison to forty years ago, ecologically minded and, as in all things human, a little crazy about it, too.

I look at the soup of the day – foggy rain, rain, rain; and I am reminded of the movie Blade Runner. It rained all the time in that supposed future. The thing about sci-fi is it tends to become reality much sooner than it was portrayed as happening. The writer's fiction is often outpaced by reality; predictions get beaten to the punch by the pace of 'real' life.

I think of this spring's record-setting rains, and I remember the torrents of last October, which flooded out Southern New Hampshire, and last spring's heavier-than-usual pounding of rain, and I think now I'm a believer in the planetary warming, greenhouse effect. Not that there ever was a serious question about it; it's been evident for quite some time.

The weather patterns have been altered and seem to be heading into a dreary Blade Runner future.

Reality overtakes science fiction portrayals and predictions once more.

Riding the T: Don't I Know You?

You never know who you might run into riding the subway or what they might say.

"Excuse me? Don't I know you?"

"I don't think so…"

"You write songs?"

"No."

"Oh… Well, hiya doing? I got my headphones, learning my parts." (His hands feign drumming strokes.)

"You're a drummer?"

"Yep."

"Me too. I played in bands from high school to my mid-30s."

"Don't I know you? Maybe working through Baystate?

"No, I don't think so, but I'm looking for work, including through Baystate."

"I knew a drummer named Phil who worked at Baystate."

"My name is Phil, and I'm a drummer, but I never worked at Baystate."

"So, what are you writing?"

"Short stories and poetry."

"I went to Berklee in '76."

"Well, you know, I went to the New England Conservatory of Music in 1977, and

1978. The same part of town, maybe we met back then…"

"You were a friend of Ed Schuller, hung at Michael's jazz club on Gainsborough Street."

"How do you know that?"

"I remember you. You were skinnier then."

"Yeah, I was on dope then."

"What did you do at NEC?"

"A lot of dope."

"Naw. For real."

"I was a composition major, percussion minor. I wrote symphonic, jazz and third-stream

music. Do you play in a band?

"Yeah, I'm at Wally's tonight. So, you write stories, poems?"

"Yeah, it's kind of funny musically; I almost never wrote words, now that's all I write.

Maybe someday, for fun, I'll stick 'em together and surprise myself."

"I knew I knew you. Well, anyway, I'm at Wally's tonight."

"Jazz jam?"

"Yup."

"Sorry to say I can't get free tonight. I have a meeting I'm going to; I'm trying to stay sober. But anyway, good seeing you again."

"Nice to see you, Phil."

"Wandering on my ruinous walk

by the dial stone aged and green

one rose of the wilderness left on its stalk

to mark where a garden had been."

-Campbell

Bessie In the Kitchen

I wish I could plant music in my house

and around my yard like people who garden,

and grow flowers and plants.

I'd sculpt a hedge of the Muddy Waters

The band along Route 111 at the far edge of the

front yard as a barrier to traffic noise.

I'd put James Booker in the coat room,

place Professor Longhair in the

hallways and closets.

Plant Bill Evans along the driveway,

seed the garden with Charles Mingus

and Jimi Hendrix's blues, along with

Howlin' Wolf and Tom Waits

lead pipe grays.

Bessie Smith in the kitchen, arms reach

from the pig feet and beer.

Stevie Ray Vaughan is on the fridge.

Freddie King on the fireplace mantle.

Sonny Terry in the guest room.

Aaron Neville and Smokey Robinson

in the honey jars on the window sills.

Scrapper Blackwell in the flowerbox.

Shade in the sideyard is just right for

the Texas Nightingale Sippie Wallace.

Robert Nighthawk on the porch.

Jimmy Rogers by the Flagstones with

Sunnyland Slim, Big Maceo Merriweather,

and Little Brother Montgomery.

JB Hutto and the Hawks by the rocks.

Swing music by the duck pond.

Tommy Dorsey in the morning, The

Milkman's Matinee.

Benny Goodman's artillery later,

Duke Ellington later still.

Skip James and Blind Boy Fuller by

the flower garden. John Lee Hooker's Cookers

and Stories by the front door, Albert Collins

and the Icebreakers by the back door.

Big Joe Turner in the pantry, Otis Spann,

Johnny Shines and Elmore James in the

music room.

Barbeque Bob, alongside Laughing Charlie,

with Big Bill Broonzy over by the barbeque grill.

Little Walter Jacobs and Peetie Wheatstraw

around the patio deck with Casey Bill Weldon.

Pinetop Perkins, Koko Taylor, Tampa Red

and Washboard Sam next to the woodshed.

Billy Boy Arnold and Lillian Glinn with

Bessie in the kitchen.

Hubert Sumlin next to the little creek.

Big Joe Williams around the see-saw.

Billie Holiday in the living room.

Valerie Wellington in the dining room.

Willie Big Eyes Smith and Elgin Evans

in the breakfast room, Herbie Hancock, over

by the laundry room.

Big Walter Horton in the window box,

Willie Dixon and Carey Bell in the window

boxes, too.

Mai Kramer spinning blues on the radio.

Elizabeth Cotton, James Cotton, and

Taj Mahal lining the back fence.

Guitar Slim, Snooks Eaglin, Earl

King and Katie Webster in the sunroom:

Musique Das Freites Neveaux Orleans.

Paul Butterfield in a gutbucket,

Sonnyboy Williamson in a gut bucket, too.

Butterbeans and Susie by the vegetables,

next to Victoria Spivy Ivy.

Memphis Minnie in the playroom.

Bessie in the good ol' wagon.

Robert Johnson on the end tables,

Charlie Patten on the trail by the side fence.

Mac Rebbenack is at the piano, so is

Pete Johnson, Jimmy Yancy,

Otis Spann and Leroy Carr, too.

Willie Big Eyes Smith by the glass packs,

Elgin Evans, S.P. Leary, Francis Clay, and

Odie Payne by the sliding glass doors,

Fred Below in the soul shadows.

Pink Anderson, Kokomoe Arnold,

Lonnie Johnson, T-Bone Walker,

Johnny Winter, Lightning Hopkins,

and Sonnyboy Williamson I in the den,

with Buddy Moss, Clarence 'Gatemouth'

Brown, Blind Willie McTell, and

Skip James.

Bessie in the kitchen with Bertha 'Chippie'

Hill, Lil Green, and Clara Smith singing:

Weeping Willow Blues,

In the House Blues,

Down Hearted Blues,

Preachin' Blues,

Young Woman Blues,

blues I can use.

Clara's Bush

Clara had the sweetest little bush,

so many times I wanted simply to put

my head between her legs and munch

her. Her pheromones broadcast their

mad dance directly into the bulls-eye

of my e-zone.

Half the time that we sat in the

same room, I had a hard-on. I have never been so turned on by any

woman.

One night several years ago, I awoke

in the middle of the night to use the

toilet, as I walked by the living room

couch, I could see Clara lying on her

back asleep, as usual, but instead of

lying flat on her back, her feet were

pulled up towards her butt, knees up,

legs spread some, her pants and

underpants were pulled down below

her knees, and one hand rested on her

tummy.

It looked to me that she had

masturbated and probably had fallen

asleep after she had climaxed –

something I myself had done more

than once.

I was struck by how lovely her bush

was the opposite of some of the

tangled, humid jungles to which I'd

been, and even though I know it is a

matter of intense privacy for some,

and embarrassment, my only thoughts

and feelings, then and now, were of

how beautiful she was.

> "Wax on, wax off."
>
> Wisdom of Mr. Miyagi
>
> (From "The Karate Kid")

Mr. Miyagi Wax Off

Pitiful dreams. When I nodded off for a short nap, I dreamed I had 2 or 3 ripe snipes for smoking in my ashtray, when in real life, I had none. Nothing like dreaming big! Such are the limits of today's dreams by an insomniac nicotine addict. I need one of those back-of-the-cheap-magazine products, the type that boasts, "NEW SECRET FORMULA: 1000-year-old Indonesian cure for insomnia! Also cures smoking, ED, gallstones, headaches, toothaches, MORE!"

I got an unexpected phone call; a woman asked if she was addressing Philip Natale. I told her she was.

She didn't identify herself to me and asked if I had an appointment for March 19. I asked, "Appointment where?" She said, "North Suffolk Mental Health." I told her, "No, I don't have an appointment."

She then asked me, "Do you know Tuesday Burns?"

I didn't know any Tuesday Burns; she had to be playing games with me. I was thinking that I didn't appreciate her playing a prank at my expense. Tuesday burns – next, she was going to ask me if my refrigerator was running… I felt a little bit foolish for not picking up on it sooner.

Then it hit me; the referring doctor I saw last month for insomnia was Dr. Burns. She was supposed to get back to me a month ago, but she never did, and Dr. Burns was a woman, *Tuesday* Burns. She must have made the appointment for me, but I was never notified about it by her or her office.

No prank call after all. Jeez, am I losing it? Maybe soon I'll start sleeping. But not today. This whole post-drug-addiction traumatic stress business is wearing pretty darn thin. Sometimes, I don't know, I get surprised or startled easily, or does it just take me longer to get a handle on things? Either way, I seem susceptible to getting mixed up, muddled, or otherwise confused, at least more than normal.

The checks for the first of the month came out today, so even the biggest bums in the world and the substance abusers can shine for a few days.

Pursuant to that, people are sneaking in the back door, pounding up the stairs, down the stairs. I know exactly what they're doing. Of course, there's no secret there. They're smoking crack, shooting heroin, and doing absolutely nothing good for anybody, especially themselves.

You'd think that living in this rooming house would imperil my sobriety, but it seems to bring out a reciprocal reaction in me.

All the drug abuse behavior I see around me, here in the building and out in the square, just turns me off about the entire enterprise of getting high.

I guess being sober and sane allows me to see it as the ugly, and destructive, sad endeavor that it is.

Rather than tempting me, it only strengthens my resolve to remain sober.

In a sense, they're making like Mr. Miyagi. Mr. Miyagi wax on, Mr. Miyagi wax off, because that's all they're doing,

they're just engaging in an alternate form

of masturbation.

And making my insomnia worse.

Mai Cramer's Blues After Hours

Mai Cramer's Blues After Hours has been off the air for two decades, yet I still miss it, and I miss Mai. After all, Mai Cramer was Blues After Hours, and Blues After Hours was Mai Cramer. There simply wasn't one without the other.

She played all kinds of blues, electric blues, acoustic blues, country blues, urban blues, jump blues, rhythm and blues, rocking blues, Chicago blues, Delta blues, Memphis blues, Piedmont blues, Detroit blues, West Coast blues, 12-bar blues, piano blues, harmonica blues, dirty blues, 16-bar blues, 8-bar blues, pre-war blues, post-war blues, Italian blues, St. Louis blues, jazz blues, soul-blues, instrumental blues, deep blues, and downhome blues.

Mai had ears from Tiffany's and a 24-karat soul that shined. She loved the blues, and she loved sharing the blues.

Mai had a way of connecting us all to the music and to each other. On Friday and Saturday nights, for a few precious hours, WGBH radio became a community, a blues music lover's community.

Each one of us was a valued and special member of that community.

I don't know how she did it, but Mai managed to give the listeners individualized attention, while still working her magic over the air.

I called the station frequently, asking questions about the music, making song requests, or answering trivia questions to win tickets to blues performances. She usually answered the calls personally while still wrangling the listening community and the music.

Mai had a way of moving the program, along with her brand of affable professionalism, enthusiasm, and genuine love for the music we all shared.

Jon Garelick of the Boston Phoenix wrote, "Listeners came to Mai for her humor, her depth of knowledge, the warmth of her delivery, and her obvious passion for the music. She was a free spirit, generous, boundlessly enthusiastic, and boundlessly supportive of blues musicians." And indeed, all of those qualities were on display consistently during her twenty-four years of doing Blues After Hours, both on and off the air.

She had time for everyone, and she filled us with great music. I know from my discussions with her over the years that she was as passionate about blues music as any of us. Mai truly embraced the music and the history while keeping abreast of current events. She never failed to provide support for the bands and the players who were performing in the area or had albums out.

Mai featured what she called 'the blues calendar' at least once during each program. She compiled an extensive and up-to-date list of blues acts performing in the bars, clubs, and performance venues from Boston and

Cambridge, Worcester and Cape Cod, New Hampshire and Providence. She read the complete list over the air each night.

Mai also engendered interest by discussing which shows she had attended and sharing something about those performances with the audience. She also gave away pairs of free tickets to those various shows during every program as well.

I was often the beneficiary of those free tickets, having attended many performances, including the Taj Mahal, Ronnie Earl, and the Broadcasters Albert Collins and the Icebreakers and Marcia Ball, courtesy of Mai Cramer and WGBH radio.

The show took its name, Blues After Hours, from the great blues song of the same name. Mai opened the program each night by playing the Pinetop Perkins version of Blues After Hours and closed it out with the instrumental rendition by Lloyd Glenn.

For me, the show was most enjoyable and meaningful; it was greatly anticipated at week's end and served as a temporary respite from the unhappy marriage I was buried in.

I first embraced the blues in the fall of 1970, when I was 16. A bunch of us hung out in the evenings at a friend's house smoking weed and listening to records. One of the records we listened to was a double album called "Story of the Blues," a 1969 compilation by Columbia Records.

The album had acoustic country blues from the earliest recordings of blues in the teens and '20s. It also had urban and rural blues from the thirties, and electric blues from before World War II and after. The ordered presentation of music from the earliest era to the modern era made The Story of the Blues a good choice for a beginner like myself.

Between lyrics about hard times during the Depression, the clever and humorous double entendre; and the tales of heartache and suffering, joy and pain, good whiskey, and bad luck, I was intrigued, and I was hooked.

As much as I liked the lyrics, I was blown away by the level of musicianship. There were smoking slide guitars, and incredible pianists, harmonica players, and bass players so skilled they could have been aliens. There were singers with the voices of angels and that of gravelly-throated auctioneers.

I borrowed the album for a while so that I could listen to it and study it at home. I got to know the songs and the bands on the album and began seeking out more of their material. I also began finding updated versions of those songs that had been recorded by contemporary rock bands.

The Story of the Blues album introduced me to the blues as a genre. In turn, the blues revealed a vast treasure of music represented by many different types and styles, as it had filtered down through a century-plus of evolution across different regions of the country and along the many decades of the timeline.

That album introduced me to musicians like Charley Patton, Bessie Smith, Big Bill Broonzy, Elmore James, Otis Spann, Robert Johnson, Leroy Carr, and Scrapper Blackwell and I became a real fan of them all. But when I came across Mai Cramer's Blues After Hours, the blues of the universe that I'd been living in was greatly expanded. It was as if I'd been wading in the ocean waist-deep, and was now, diving in. I'd never heard a radio program that played such fantastic music or was as informative as Mai's.

I listened to the show and recorded it on cassette each Friday and Saturday night from 1983 until 1991, and I'm glad I did because I can listen to one of Mai's shows whenever the impulse strikes me.

Also, I'm taking all my recordings of the blues shows, and I'm recreating playlists – one for each program – on YouTube for my personal listening. And while the music's great, the playlists lack an essential ingredient, and that is the sound of Mai Cramer's voice and her words.

Some 21 years ago, a series of events, namely, long-term addiction, a serious head injury, and an eviction, had landed me in deep shit, and I was living in a homeless shelter out in Boston Harbor on Long Island. The place was called Long Island Shelter and I lived out there from July 2000 to July 2004.

It was while I lived out there that I began to turn my life around. The head injury finally healed in 2002, and in 2004, I began getting off the drugs that I'd gotten so very addicted to over the course of the previous 23 years.

Part of the process of turning my life around included surrendering myself to several local courthouses to answer default warrants that had been outstanding. Because I hadn't shown up for my court dates initially, a judge had me detained until my new court date of July 9th, 2004, which was five weeks away. He was ensuring that I'd show up on July 9. I suppose I can't really blame him, given all the times I defaulted, and so off I went.

It was when I was in jail, in the 'new man.' cellblock, in June of 2004, another inmate and fellow blues lover told me that Mai Cramer had died of cancer.

It hit me like a clean, hard punch to the solar plexus. I'd had no idea and had been out of touch with many things since my life had unraveled at the turn of the millennium.

He said he thought she'd died a couple of years earlier, but couldn't say exactly when. He said that he'd lived in the same apartment building as she, and at 90 pounds, Mai had kept fighting on and doing her thing right up until the end.

The news knocked me on my ass. I was stunned, and I was upset. It wasn't fair, and I was angry at the impossibility and cruelty of it.

I felt bad for not having known about her ordeal, even though it would have changed nothing. I wished I'd taken the time to let Mai know how much the show had meant to me back then when I was a sad young man living in Malden during the 80s.

I never missed a program. Mai's kind, and friendly, musically astute manner helped get me through the miserable hard times and the loneliness of my life in the 80's.

Talking to Mai was always such a pleasure. She was upbeat, possessing a positive nature, and she cared about her listeners.

She was a serious student of blues and R&B, and was a musicologist of high standing. She continually educated all of us in the beauty and high art of blues music.

Today, there are about seventy-five tapes of Blues After Hours from the 1980s that have survived the years, and it does my heart good to hear Mai Cramer's voice once again.

Blues Before Sunrise

I was worrying about my cigarette smoking and addiction. I wanted to quit, but at the same time, I needed to buy more. At seven dollars a pack, it's no joke.

I was peeking through my drawn blinds, when I spied the encroaching first light. I gave myself over to it, opened the blinds, and pulled them up, exposing the window in its entirety and the embryonic first light of the growing morning.

I shut off my lamp, took a seat, and watched as night gave way to predawn, and the whispering infinite blues, washing up from dead east, as the day's light ever so gradually grew.

Brilliant splashes of color grabbed the nearly invisible clouds as surely as paint grabs a brush in a changing, kaleidoscopic free-for-all.

Long swaths of ocean cumulus hug the coastline sky here each morning in winter and appear in succession as loosely arranged stripes along the ocean's horizon from north to south. They serve as canvas for the morning light, which colors the sky with quiet, watery blues, while igniting the clouds in dazzling bright hues.

This morning features three wide, brash stripes of blazing red van Gogh brushstrokes, sitting below three more extraordinary raspberry rungs of cool fire.

Without ego or the need to be anything, the sky ultimately explodes in heavenly blues, purples, reds, and oranges, and all this changing color happens in stark stone silence.

The sun of millions upon millions of atomic

and hydrogen bombs rises forth as we spin into a dancing position in the great cosmic conduction.

While early colors bleed out to an apparently overcast, dim purple/gray day, the fireball orange of the rising sun sings the far horizon. It creates a series of brilliantly vivid-yellow, north-to-south, short-lived stripes as the purple swizzles and drains from the overcast canopy.

It leaves a dark gray that presents a faint tinge of indigo and blue, while the increasing light of the day illuminates only the darkness of heavy clouds and squeezes the orange and red of sunrise into the thin horizontal window between well-lit rooftops and the wintertime ocean cumulus above them that ride over the Atlantic.

Today's installment of first light's morning show doesn't disappoint; in fact, it dazzles.

Angelina's Lips

Sorry, Angelina, you're beautiful, but…

The photo of Angelina Jolie in the Boston Globe and in newspapers the country over was a promo ad for the 2008 Clint Eastwood movie, 'Changeling.' It's quite a photo. Who has lips like that? I must assume that as the result of careful makeup and lighting, as well as Jolie's natural comportment and the careful camera angle, we arrive at this pic.

In this photo, Angelina, decked out in beige on beige, with a beige ornament on her beige lapel, a low-slung chocolate brown hat that reveals only some of her brown eyebrows that stride atop her pale blue eyes, and just a solo brunette curl on either side – an inscrutable gaze and impeccably neat attire – is all about lips.

Her lips are huge and very red and almost frightening. They look like cauliflower lips.

One could execute a one-and-a-half twist, double somersault dive into a swimming pool off of her bottom lip. That is, as long as you stood far enough out so that you didn't bang your head on her upper lip in your springboard-like ascent.

The photo reminds me of those made-for-Halloween wax lips – those oversized wax lips with the stick you insert between your teeth to hold the lips in place over your mouth.

If you put the photo next to a shot of Jack Nicholson as the smiling Joker in 'Batman,' you'd have a matching set.

In short, it's too much. This is the Hustler magazine beaver shot of lips. Too much is always too much.

Lips are very sensuous, yes, and Angelina's lips are normally luscious. But when you exaggerate too much, the sensuality is lost to grotesque obviousness. Nobody likes obviousness. To kiss the girl in this photo is to risk that she'll suck your face off.

Perhaps because it is October 24th, Clint Eastwood is pulling a Hollywood Halloween gag.

The Ashes of Failure

He'll be walking out into a heavy

snowstorm in the morning, but

tonight, he'll stay in during the stormy,

long winter night.

He's glad he has tobacco,

he'll be snug like a bug in a rug,

comfortable, content, by himself.

He'd rather have a partner,

but that's a luxury,

a difficult bill to fill.

The snow and wind fly

outside of his door, but

the world is not strapped upon his back,

and his mouth is no longer full of

the ashes of failure.

His brain isn't rolling the bad breaks

around in neon,

like a one-armed bandit

tripling the lemons.

He's not wanting for a home,

he has a place, his own spot,

it's not the Ritz, but it's also not

a homeless shelter; it's right

where he belongs today.

Tomorrow, in the deep snow,

he'll stand above the ashes of failure;

tomorrow, in the blinding snow,

it'll be a good day.

Early Recovery Days

Crimson sharks swim the tide,

that has long since turned;

I stroke carefully the holdover

dreams of yesterday,

gingerly cradle, and gently,

smooth out a life returned,

from the absurd.

Birthday Happy Birthday

The apples are spilled before the cart

for all to see, a worm in everyone. The

horse is in the tree, while sugar-free

women on the prowl rip away at the

songs that silence the night darken the

soul, do re mi, don't count on me,

yeah, rip it, baby,

I know you,

listen to me, sol, la, ti,

do, ti, lasso my balls,

while you write me:

a check that won't cash,

a song that won't play,

a card that won't mail, on

an occasion no one remembers,

meanwhile, I endured,

my candle burns brightly,

finally, on the other side of

50-plus: a few dings and scratches,

just needs a little paint,

got new tires,

low mileage, seems even lower,

it's got forward, reverse is tricky,

straight on is best,

not a guzzler,

runs on regular,

all original parts,

it's got a big back seat,

pressure's been checked,

just give me a little push,

as I myself, write

an early birthday card,

from the heart,

to myself.

      Pen me in the noble hero,

to the top of the tree,

top of the gnarled apple tree,

where I'm forever 10 years old;

to the top of the moon,

where I'm sad and alone, to the top of tomorrow,

where I'll yet do my best work.

   Now write me in,

I'll take my place,

right next to all the other ghosts,

while I gather my own specters,

who aren't so many,

but we make up for it,

singing, re, mi, fa, fa, sol, fa,

so good, so long.

* A fifty-third birthday present to myself. *

Ashes of Failure Too

In Chelsea's Bellingham Square, he watches the people chew on the ashes of failure, and it accumulates in the streets like snow from a blizzard.

He knocks it off his shoes before he goes into his home and wipes it from his eyes. A trail of ash leads down the hall, all the way into John's room, where a woman injects herself in the neck, while looking in a mirror, and in the foot, between the toes.

He can taste the ash as he walks past on the way to his room; she's a decent soul in her forties, whose eyes look to be one hundred, and tired from the pounding.

He recognizes the condition of battle fatigue and shell shock, the resultant effects when far too many bad things have occurred consistently over a long period of time.

At some point, he knows there'll be some kind of breakdown, a meltdown that occurs when the mind and the nervous system refuse to believe and cannot, in any normal sense, cope with it.

The brain blows a gasket and remains in shock from being asked to process far too much trauma, excessive brutality, too many horrific surprises, and too much bad luck.

It's a safe mode, possibly an alternative to stripping naked and running through the city screaming like a banshee.

It's emotional exhaustion, mental incomprehension, and spiritual destitution.

Next door, it's the crack pipe and heroin, and whatever else, and more ash piling up.

Outside his window, crack and alcohol use is visible, and the ashes of failure swirl while the wind churns in circles around the back lot.

Instead of temptation, he finds that all the people getting high in the building and around the square only sets him firmer on his path of sobriety.

In the bad weather, and in winter, the homeless junkies ask to come in out of the cold. He talks to Jackie now and then and feels comfortable letting him come in when it's cold, ignoring the ash until he leaves, then promptly sweeps it out.

Jackie likes alcohol, methadone, and Klonopin. When he's feeling frisky, he has the younger ones get him crack and heroin.

At 62, he's bent over and brain-addled. His legs are practically gangrene, and his big hands are perpetually swollen.

He is 6 foot four, and weighs nearly 250, so, it's unlikely he'll get ripped off, except when he's deeply nodded out.

When he first met Jackie and his wife, he was startled by their appearance, which was generally broken down and stupefied due to decades of rampant drug abuse. The ashes of failure were chokingly thick on them and around them.

Over time, he's become desensitized to Jackie's demeanor and appearance, although he can still be unpleasantly surprised from time to time. But there's something about Jackie that he likes nonetheless.

Recently, when he was ordering a sub sandwich to go, Jackie had come into the sub shop to get sandwiches for his wife and himself. He was trailing ash all over the floor, and as usual, he was bent over, eyelids half-closed, and appearing as if he might tip over.

It was nearly 11 pm, and Jackie was trashed. His big hands, looking like two beat-up balls of meat with vague knuckles, were shaking.

Jackie claimed his hands and fingers had been broken in a vise many years ago as punishment for not losing a boxing match in the correct round.

Waiting for his order, he saw the stares and looks of revulsion that Jackie was getting from the other sub-shop patrons. He guessed they were fueled by the same shock he experienced when he first met Jackie. After all, one just doesn't see big, gnarled, and raggedy figures all covered in ash, such as Jackie, every day.

The stares made him a bit uncomfortable, and he imagined they might make Jackie uncomfortable, too.

Even when he's high as a kite, Jackie is surprisingly aware, and he wonders if it bothers the big guy, being the target of those stares, or if he's immune to it.

Jackie writes poetry, and says he would rather have been a poet instead of a boxer.

But the one thing Jackie's never talked about is the fact that he suffers from a case of severe addiction.

It's sad we almost never become what our hearts long to be. If we were encouraged to follow with our brains where our hearts led, there might be fewer addicts and far less ash on the streets.

It Should All Be Like Church

The man in the red hat said everyone on the island was getting their social security check this morning.

There's always somebody saying that the Social Security checks are coming early this month. I swear there is! Yet, in ten years or 120 months, I've never once gotten mine early. Never. They always come when they are supposed to come.

I said to the guy in the red hat, "Not me, but I'll get mine next week."

He said, "My check was taken. Warrants. Felony warrants. Drugs."

"Me too. But I got mine back."

"How did you do that?"

"I surrendered; cleaned up my cases."

"Mine are in California. I can't get there."

"Surrender to the authorities."

"They don't want me; won't take me back there."

"Maybe a journalist could prompt or embarrass the authorities into bringing you back?"

"Then they'd hammer me, stick me in jail for a long time."

"I see what you mean… but you'd have legal representation."

"I pled guilty."

"I surrendered. In Cambridge, on 06/06/06, no less. They knew I was sober, had no arrests and been out of trouble five years. They let me walk on personal – Hey! What did you say? You took a guilty already?"

" Yeah."

"What's the warrant for? Jumping probation?"

"No, I picked up a new charge."

"And so, you jumped probation, too?"

"Yeah."

"California. That's a tough one. But I'd find a way to get there."

"This country has seen an increase in felony arrests by a factor of times 7."

"I believe it, and I suspect that people are pretty much the same as always. Tougher laws."

"Yeah."

"They have a legal drug zone in Vancouver, B.C., that includes SIS – Supervised Injection Sites"

"I used to live there. Europe has them, too."

"Yeah. Switzerland, Great Britain. Europeans are more enlightened about drugs. Maybe they can afford to be, and there's far less violence there. All of the U.K. has fewer murders than Beantown. You could throw in Switzerland's murder rate, too."

"Yeah. This fucking country, it's a police state."

"I used to worry about that; I longed to be in the U.K. or Switzerland. I don't worry about it anymore, though."

"There's always a new push from somewhere for another drug crackdown."

"People don't want drugs, or drug treatment programs, in their neck of the woods. There's enough violence associated with it so that people look at it all the same: Drugs equals violence and crime."

(silence)

"My case in Cambridge was drugs. Social Security took my checks for a felony warrant. That's why I'm here."

"Did you shoot heroin?"

"No. Well, yeah, when I was very young. I broke my neck at 27, got addicted to pain pills; a year of that, and they said, 'we're putting you on a methadone clinic.' I stayed there 21-plus years. 2 ½ years ago I walked, cold turkey, off it, and one month later I walked, the same way, off of valiums and Klonopin. My life is good. Sorry, I don't mean to sound like a preacher."

"Church. It all should be like church: Where you can go to let your wife sing, and sleep while she does!"

(Cracks me up) *"That's* funny."

On the Brink of Distinction

I had seen the man during the four weeks that I'd been at Long Island shelter. He was in a heavy-duty neck brace and had the raggedy, greasy look of a hard-nosed drinker and drugger. He was beaten up, defeated, and eminently qualified to be squashed dead like a bug by life. He had the demeanor of someone who'd removed himself far from the scene of the crime – in this case, the crime being his own life.

He had a load of jailhouse tattoos. Not the fashionable, regular tattoos you see every day, but the type acquired in a jail or prison. He had enough so that they covered every square inch of both arms from the wrists up to his short sleeves.

Where he'd attained those tattoos spoke to where he had learned how to remove himself and where he'd learned to kill time. In that sense, I suppose just about everybody in jail is a killer.

Still, he'd learned the lesson far too well. Carrying that perverse practice beyond jail and into the real world is dangerous because it all but guarantees a trivial, tedious existence.

If not fucked for life, he was definitely fucked for the time being. Time wasn't his friend, as he hurtled breakneck toward his death. Demise was a constant companion. He was a bomb whose arming device had malfunctioned, and he wasn't detonating, ever. But why should I be so affected by this guy, so repulsed?

The truth was that many things about him reminded me

beyond a flirtation of myself not so very long ago, and the reminiscence was not pleasurable. Much about the years I spent out at Long Island Shelter was brought to mind by him.

That guy in the neck brace made me wonder how I must have looked to the other riders when I was riding the subways to get out of the winter cold before I was in recovery. I stayed at the shelter each night from their 5 pm opening until 6 am when they closed their doors for the day. During the daytime, in the winter, I rode the subways to stay warm.

I can remember the looks of pity and genuine sorrow on the other riders' faces sometimes when I woke up from sleeping, or from a nod. At times, I heard remarks between riders about me, like, 'what a shame,' or 'How sad.'

Riding the trolleys as a kid, when there was a wino or a derelict on board, I remember that people would remark about the unfortunate soul in much the same way. Many years later, I was that derelict, and it wasn't as far of a walk as people think.

I had to wonder what else I had in common with the guy in the neck brace. We both had lived at Long Island Shelter in Boston, both had worn neck braces, and we both had suffered problems with substance abuse. With commitment and hard work, I had put myself on the road to recovery, but it appeared to be a long way off before he might achieve the same.

I was glad that our positions weren't reversed, as he was still using and living out at the shelter. But my content was strangely qualified. I was glad, like a child wrongfully accused of dipping into the cookie jar, who can say truthfully of this occasion, "Not me," but is aware of all the times he had taken cookies and just hadn't been caught. But still, I was doing well in my recovery, and there was no need to run myself down. I guess having to go back to the shelter for four weeks was a bit of a blow to my self-esteem. But it had to be done until my reinstated SSDI checks started coming in again.

My circumstantial doppelganger was paired up with a somewhat younger, good-looking blonde. She wasn't, as of yet, wearing that look of tired, broken-down pessimism, with the 'fuck-you-eyes' that some of the guests out at the homeless shelter seem to wear.

As far as I could tell, she was loyal and attentive. She would, from time to time, engage in polite small talk with whoever might be at her table in the cafeteria, and from time to time, engage in polite small talk with whoever might be at her table in the cafeteria or sitting nearby her in the front yard. He, on the other hand, never spoke. So, I was surprised when he got up off his perch and approached me one day, and spoke up. "How long before you were able to move your head side-to-side, like this, and like this?"

Obviously, he'd overheard another island resident and me discussing broken necks, surgeries, and Halo braces the other day. On the strength of hearing that discussion, he was familiar with part of my orthopedic history, particularly the fractured cervical spine and fusion part of it.

He had questions, so I tried to satisfy his curiosity by answering them thoroughly. He didn't say much in reply, and I was thinking that by the time he spoke again, I might be long gone and hard to find. I'd be leaving the island for normal civilization in a few days when my check came in.

****

I hadn't seen the neck brace guy since I was at the shelter six months ago. But he sprouted up overnight like a mushroom, appearing in my neighborhood in Chelsea one morning, selling newspapers. There he was with a stack of Heralds and the same blonde who was with him on the island.

It was quite a coincidence that this fellow, who'd elicited such strong feelings in me out at Long Island, should show up in my hometown, in my neighborhood. If I didn't know better, I'd think somebody up there wasn't done with me regarding this particular lesson.

The first few days that he was selling The Herald on the Bellingham Square traffic island, I noticed that he and his girlfriend looked skinnier and a bit more beat-up than last spring on Long Island. But that wasn't surprising, given their lifestyle.

The traffic island had the potential to support a permanent, full-time newsstand, but the big question was whether the city would allow it. One would have to inquire at the city's code enforcement bureau to determine if a permit or license was required. But it seemed that he might be onto a good thing with commitment and hard work.

He'd adjourned from selling the newspapers for the long Christmas weekend, then resumed the following Tuesday morning. It was early in the morning when I spotted him selling his newspapers in the square, and I tried to talk to him like a regular guy. It was going okay until he said he had a 50-million-dollar lawsuit against the California prison system and added, "But I've got to be out there to get it." It was then that all the red flags went up, and my bullshit meter started flashing wildly.

I said if that were the situation, he'd have no trouble finding a local attorney to handle it. He replied, "Well, they'd have to keep flying out there." I said, "For one-third of 50 million dollars, they will. Or hook up with a lawyer out in California. For a third of fifty million, an Eskimo lawyer would take it." But of course, he doesn't have a case for 50 million dollars. If he did, he'd be tending to it.

I was disappointed. I had worked hard at not disliking the guy after many very bad impressions. I had even taken issue with myself for rushing to judgment on the guy. But then he hits me with this ragtime about a big-money lawsuit that's nothing but wishful thinking on his part. In the future, it'll be best to keep him at arm's length. I don't want to work up the dislike I had for him initially. It's negative, and it's not healthy for the bearer. Besides, he'll probably disappear from the neighborhood as quickly as he'd appeared.

Another thing is, on that morning; unfortunately, his eyes were pinned, so it wasn't unlikely that he was relapsing. Quite possibly, on his road, it would become very tough sledding real soon.

Redemption and Reclamation

Gay Brewer has written a very good book for Twaynes' United States Author Series, "Charles Bukowski." Better than the other biographies, essays, and studies on Bukowski that I've read thus far, Brewer's work is even-handed, thorough, and thoughtful.

Brewer says that much of Charles Bukowski's work is largely redemptive and about personal reclamation, and he's absolutely right. When you consider that he claims the poem was Bukowski's lifeline to sanity, the sentiment about redemption and reclamation is an understatement. For Buke, it was either write poems or go mad.

When you've spent a lifetime with the creative craze, and you're anti-social -not fitting in not earning dollars - you need some redemptionc. Redemption in the form of doing something well can do the trick. Any reclamation of the daily events you can muster in the meantime goes a long way, too. In some cases, it's the difference between intolerable madness and the kind that you can cope with, and that difference can be one of degree and, in the end, the difference between life and early death.

I thank God for Charles Bukowski, and if I read Gay Brewer correctly, he does, too.

Staving off madness with written reclamation? Yes. Redemption through art? You know it.

I only wish I knew how to stave off starvation and poverty through writing and art. Or at least, I wish I'd started writing about thirty-five years earlier.

Here's one for you, Buke.

Hope and Fear

I had a secret fear that the hope I carried was futile. I feared my hope would never see the light of day or come to fruition.

It was the hope that I'd one day be free of homelessness, free of the shelter, and free of the misery that was my life, and that hope was crucial to my survival and sanity.

Without it, the entire ordeal might have been beyond my ability to cope, and if that were the case, there's no telling what may have followed. I can't rule out the possibility that madness or suicide could have been the result. But even with the hope I maintained, I probably wasn't far from either eventuality.

I called it a secret fear because I kept it hidden from myself as much as possible, out of my mind and outside of my belief system.

It amounted somewhat to a game I played with myself, for how can one completely discount and disregard an idea once it has been thought of? It would be like trying to un-ring a bell. The best I could do, as a matter of trying to stay positive, was to shove it aside. I kept my fear as small as possible, as tucked away and hidden as possible.

It was somewhat tricky business making a conscious effort to keep thoughts as far out of my mind as possible. The effort itself tended to suggest the very thing I was trying to avoid thinking about. It became a somewhat Zen-like enterprise. But whatever way it was accomplished, it was important not to lose the hope that I'd one day be out of the shelter.

The thought that I was never going to get back to having a home of my own and that homelessness was my permanent condition was simply unacceptable. The eventuality was too grim for me to consider, too heavy to bear.

I knew that it was, indeed, possible to become a permanent member of the homeless contingent. I had only to look around at many of the faces I'd come to know at the shelter. There were people who'd been guests of the shelter for five, ten, and twenty years. Most of those long-term people had given up any thought of living in their own homes. There was no effort in that direction on their part and no apparent hope or discussion about it. They'd been homeless for a very long time, and somewhere along the line it had simply become a way of life.

The idea of becoming permanently homeless was too awful for me to contemplate. If that fear had taken root, it would have been equivalent to having no hope whatsoever. It would have stood before me as a taunt, a jibe; the fear would have twisted hope into a barefaced lie, a painful and costly delusion.

It's simply how I felt about it then. Looking back, I suppose the whole thing was about trying to stay positive and not let the enormity of my predicament overwhelm and defeat me. Fear can be infectious, so I needed to keep calm. It was critical to keep that fear as far from my thoughts as possible.

At the same time, I kept my hope rather low-key. I didn't bubble over with it, and it didn't fill my dreams at night. I held my hopes quietly but hungrily, cautiously yet resiliently.

It helped me put one foot in front of the other, especially first thing in the morning when I could barely face another day of walking the streets.

I did my best to achieve a quiet, hassle-free existence until I could once again reenter the safety of the shelter each day at five p.m.

I wasn't always sure, back then, that I would ever see life again from beyond Boston's Long Island shelter.

Turns out I have.

PHILIP W. NATALE, III

Needle Freaks

Uneasy vampires hunting themselves,

impaling themselves with steel,

milking life's blood with a spike,

the measured pull of the plunger,

the dizzying rush of the extraction,

transfusing that thick, sticky stuff,

in and out, and in and out,

a sickly solo dance,

loading,

addition by subtraction,

a whole other breed of cat

from the sniffers, smokers, and swallowers,

and if they go long enough, slow enough,

pulling lines out of their arms,

like fishermen pulling monofilament,

long strings of coagulated blood,

running from the hole in their arm,

to the just-removed needle, which

is still in their hand but 2 feet away,

as they set it down on the table,

working at it patently silent,

among the other horrified hypes,

but working at it mostly alone,

for the pain of embarrassment,

and correctly perceived disgust,

sitting anything but pretty,

lost in a cocaine trance,

of living death and death itself,

coming to a bad end quickly,

grotesque and mean.

The Final Scene: The King of New York's Strings Are Cut

The king puppet,

his soul dipped in madness,

a ghetto shaman,

more vicious than most,

seated in his taxicab coffin,

his hand and arm dropping,

down at the elbow,

in a last conducting stroke,

a final farewell gesture,

to the uncompromising strings,

he was now and forever,

communicating with the dead,

as the whole world,

closed in for a look.

I Can feel the Darkness

The darkness at the end of the tunnel approaches,

the impossible black-marble future;

the heart that aches for a safe landing,

dashed hopes,

was it delusion?

Gouts of terrible bloody rejection,

hip deep where I walk:

hope should carry the death penalty,

the death of coming in second place,

every time, every day, every life.

Sadness too terrible to contemplate,

to face the ache that's trapped in my breast,

which feels as permanent as nuclear winter,

and as impossible as lost hell found.

All the places in the world become pointless,

all the people in the world are indifferent,

all the birthdays are forgotten,

all the deaths unobserved – except mine,

which is cheered and prayed for by me,

most of all.

The Waning Snow Moon

The moon parked far up into the night,

high, and a whisker past full,

this February snow moon is a pale-face,

a distant, cold spotlight alone,

no stars for companions on this eve, as

the night is moderately overcast and

and a murky, semi-transparent gauze

of thin, low clouds swirled fog-like,

underneath chunks of thick, black billows,

which laid like giant flagstone walkways

all across the vast North Shore sky,

and sometimes hiding this snow moon.

The cloudy sky is a jigsaw puzzle,

nearly completed but with pieces missing.

Mice, it's thought, have run off with

many puzzle pieces – those meesses –

do they think they are moon cheese pieces?

Sitting high in the sky, our snow moon

brightly illuminates the jigsaw puzzle clouds

that are whizzing by, darting and dashing

across the pale-face winter moon,

keeping the moon fully visible half the time,

but that percentage is furiously diminishing

as puzzle pieces continue filling the

game board sky, but before it dives for cover.

Our snow moon blazes and dazzles,

a jack-o-lantern candle burning fast and

brilliantly behind the carved pumpkin-teeth, scurrying clouds.

The nearly-assembled jigsaw pumpkin puzzle is still missing

pieces, allowing us

to see this hide-and-seek snow moon –

this sneak and peek rascal – a bit longer.

If only some people could likewise

disappear, or at least disappear

their bad attitude and grousing,

he would love to disappear for a

time, riding high upon the snow moon,

returning promptly by lunchtime,

the following day, for his medication,

a geriatric Peter Pan with ideals

not nearly so high as his blood pressure,

and the cholesterol, the triglycerides.

He's now been divorced far longer,

than the years he'd been married,

long enough to be okay with it,

something he never thought to achieve;

the kids are grown, the sewn seeds are delivered

to market, while the x-missile calls

occasionally, when she's particularly pilled

or drunk and angry at him, which she has

been since they met over 30 years ago,

which informs of her lack of self-control,

and he is okay with that, too, as the snow

the moon is okay with its hide-and-seek role,

and monthly appearing and disappearing acts,

but there's always tomorrow night, and

the night after that, for shining clearly,

even if then the moon has waned or waxed,

a bit more, it will still shine brightly after all of the waxing and
waning are what moons do

Composer

I am the piano that is slightly out of tune,

playing dissonant, faraway music remote,

that lies between the lines and underneath words,

a perspective less often heard,

an eaves-drop into mystical conversations,

a peep into foreign affairs,

within dimensions not entirely familiar,

stretching yet further, searching,

ever reaching outward

until, finally, the leash snaps taut

recognizing sounds that I'd heard,

that couldn't be had from there,

when I was in tune,

existing quietly hidden only,

in the thin air between my ears,

my private lasso,

tying the two together in my mind's ear,

a measuring stick editing

harmony and transposing time,

gravity pulling me toward tuned pitches past,

offering a bridge to when last they were

conventionally level, plumb, and square,

largely more accepted and loved,

than the quaint, distant cousins,

who are so very beautiful,

revealing, and so vital but,

who, to ears inexperienced or unprepared,

are elusive at best.

The Icebreaker Guitar Raker

Albert Collins, the Icebreaker and guitar raker extraordinaire, was a powerful guitarist with a unique style. He was flat-out a guitar genius who inspired the generation of Texas guitarists that followed him. In several interviews, the late, great Jimi Hendrix cites Albert Collins as an influence.

He wailed on his Telecaster as if his life depended on it, and the way he put his heart and soul into his playing was rare and inimitable. He was as fast and inventive as he wanted to be; it seemed he knew virtually no limitations.

His solo choices were always logical and refreshing, and he had an uncanny ability to play the unexpected. His bold and innovative playing surprised and delighted audiences all over the world.

Rather than the usual and the expected, Collins was adept and clearly comfortable delivering alternative and substitute riffs, chords, and passages.

He had a habit of holding a note for an extended time, bending it, and working it over with vibrato before resolving and releasing it.

Without a doubt, Albert had the magic touch, and his playing electrified me. The best way to enjoy Albert's mastery was to see him live. Seeing Albert Collins and the Icebreakers live was a spiritual and uplifting experience.

He played solos with mindful abandon, letting loose joyful, soaring figures of notes with a symmetry all his own. They'd build in intensity, climaxing with his sonic, screeching guitar leading the band back into the groove.

Collins was a natural at playing funk; indeed, his playing was inherently funky. He possessed precision and high-order dexterity matched by few guitarists. He was a blues man and a blues player through and through.

Rolling Stone ranked Albert #56 among the 100 greatest guitarists. Born in Leona, Texas, on October 1, 1932, Albert was introduced to the guitar at an early age by his cousin, blues guitarist Lightnin' Hopkins.

When his family moved to Houston in 1941, Albert grew up in the city's Third Ward area with Johnny "Guitar" Watson and Johnny "Clyde" Copeland. When he was 9, Albert took piano lessons, but when his piano tutor was unavailable, his cousin Wilson Young would lend him his guitar. He is credited with teaching young Albert the altered tuning he would use throughout his career.

Collins decided to concentrate on guitar after hearing the album "Boogie Chillen" by John Lee Hooker when he was 16. At 18, he started his group, the Rhythm Rockers, in which he honed his craft.

In 1954, at 22, Collins was joined in the Rhythm Rockers by 17-year-old Johnny Copeland, who had just left the Dukes of Rhythm.

He started to play regularly in Houston, and by the mid-1950s, he had established his reputation as a local guitarist of note. He had started to appear regularly at Walter's Lounge with the group Big Tiny and the Thunderbirds. The saxophonist and music teacher Henry Hayes heard about Collins from Joe "Guitar" Hughes. After seeing him perform live, Hayes encouraged Collins to record a single for Kangaroo Records, a label he had started with his friend M. L. Young. Collins recorded his debut single, "Freeze", backed by "Collin's Shuffle" at Gold Star Studios in Houston in the spring of 1958, with Hayes on sax.

Texas blues bands of the period used a horn section, and Collins later credited Hayes with teaching him how to arrange for horns. From 1958 to 1972, Albert recorded a string of singles and albums for small labels in Texas and California. It was after meeting the members of Canned Heat in Houston in

In June 1968, Collins decided to move to California after being advised that they could help him secure an agent and introduce him to Imperial Records.

With the offer of a record deal and regular live work, Collins moved to Palo Alto, California, in November 1968. By the spring of 1969, the move to Cali was paying off, with Albert establishing himself as a regular act on the west coast circuit.

In 1978, Bruce Iglauer, owner of Alligator Records, signed

Collins to a recording contract, beginning Albert's eight-year run of recording outstanding albums with the Icebreakers for Alligator.

From 1978 to 1986, Collins recorded six albums for Alligator Records: Ice Pickin', Frostbite, Frozen Alive, Don't Lose Your Cool, Live in Japan, and Cold Snap. As good as those albums are, seeing Albert Collins and the Icebreakers live was the ultimate Albert Collins experience.

Nobody went home from one of his performances disappointed or shortchanged. Around the time Albert Collins signed his record deal with Alligator, his wife Gwen was able to talk him into returning to a career in music full-time.

It's a shame that a hugely gifted artist like Albert Collins has to abandon his music to drive a truck or work a construction job to make ends meet. But that is exactly the predicament Collins found himself in.

In his early days, Collins worked as a paint mixer and a truck driver to put food on the table. In 1971, when he was 39 years old, he still worked in construction because he couldn't make a proper living from his music. Ironically, one of his construction jobs was a remodeling project for Neil Diamond.

He continued in this kind of work until his mid-40s when success with his Alligator Records deals finally afforded him a reliable income.

Albert was a first-rate songwriter who penned many outstanding songs, such as "MasterCard" and "Snowed In."

He had an exceptional singing voice that was more than up to the task of singing the many notable songs that he wrote. A veteran bandleader, Albert got the most from his band each night and did it without burning them out.

As a guitarist, his signature attack on the strings was 'martele', which literally means "hammered." It's a percussive stroke and a term typically used in relation to bowed stringed instruments, like violins, but it perfectly describes the hammered attack Albert uses.

His attack and the tone he wielded made Collins an easily identifiable and unique guitarist.

His ability to attack a string *'martele'* and then employ a glissando was his device. His glissando, or sliding along a string that quickly reaches the destination note he then sustained in tremolo, bolstered by a wah-wah pedal, was truly an Albert Collins trademark.

He utilized modern electric guitar's benefits, without losing his sense of the blues. His works were always grounded in the blues, and he stretched and dazzled within that genre.

He was a consummate professional who always worked hard for his audience.

Albert Collins died shortly after appearing at the House of Blues in Harvard Square, Cambridge, MA. I saw his appearance there, and his playing was fresh and inspired.

I was blown away. I could scarcely believe just how good he was. That such a force was soon after that silenced by death seemed almost impossible and was shocking. It was particularly sad because Albert had worked so hard for so long and was finally getting to enjoy success at a high level. But alas, it wasn't to be for very long…

Mr. Collins left many hours of recorded material for us to continue to enjoy. If you want to hear sharp, lively electric blues, listen seriously to Albert Collins and the Icebreakers.

The Blues Missile

"Why the keening sounds from Mississippi should strike notes of thrill, terror, and wonder in hearts in the suburbs of London, I don't know. It can only be because it goes beyond color and blood – it goes to the bone. Maybe that's it. If you look closely at the marrow, there's a little blue in there."

- Keith Richards on the influence blues had on him. From an interview in Rolling Stone, May 25, 1998, by Anthony Decurtis.

Shot like a missile out of the 1960's & 70's rock music, the blues was by the 1980's the most legitimate, happening American music on the scene. It was a poignant case of having the favor returned, given that the classic rockers grew up listening to the blues greats and were significantly influenced by them. Undoubtedly, the renewed interest in blues was brought about by the classic rock bands playing from the blues catalog. A whole new generation was exposed to blues, including the musicians of that generation.

The renewed interest in blues gave birth to bands that played a new take on blues called blues-rock and gave birth to an entire wing or subgenre of rock music called southern rock.

Led by bands such as the Allman Brothers Band, Lynyrd Skynyrd, Jackson Brown, and ZZ Top, these bands presented the blues pieces in a new, long-form doing the very thing Benny

Goodman, for instance, mostly resisted – letting the songs extend and stretch out, which allowed the various instrumentalists to take extended solos.

The new blues-rock bands of the 1970s took those blues songs and made them something new by incorporating them into their rock sensibilities, including extended song versions or jams. Those extended, improvised solos were, in this generation, handled primarily by electric guitars and keyboards mostly, rather than the woods and brass of the jazz bands.

By 1980, while rock was largely trying to reinvent itself and deciding where to go, blues was the destination of many of the great electric guitar players. Starting with Eric Clapton and Stevie Ray Vaughan, the blues attracted the tour-de-force guitarists.

Jazz employed the blues, folk used the blues, and classic rock had elements of the blues, but now the blues was speaking for itself. People were discovering Robert Johnson and Big Bill Broonzy, Memphis Minnie, and Memphis Slim. They listened to Muddy, T-Bone, B.B., Freddie, and Albert King.

The English rock bands of the 1960s, like Cream and Led Zeppelin, helped put the music of the American bluesman back onto the map and into the ears of a new generation of music lovers.

Longtime bluesmen like Hound Dog Taylor and the House Rockers, Lightning Hopkins, Sonny Terry and Brownie McGhee,

Buddy Guy, and Junior Wells were in demand and gigging again.

On the radio, blues shows of every sort popped up all over the dial. I might hear one of the new generations of players like Joe Louis Walker, Robert Ward, Sue Foley, or Robert Cray, or veterans like Muddy Waters, John Lee Hooker, or Sleepy John Estes, depending on which station I had on. But regardless of who was performing, one thing was clear: blues was alive and kicking with vibrancy and a newfound respect like never before.

Keith Jarrett Lets It Rip

Reading 'This Day in History,' I saw it was the birthday of extraordinary pianist Keith Jarrett. It was the eighth of May 2008, and according to the paper, he was turning 63. It was also the year that the pianist-composer would be inducted into the Downbeat Hall of Fame.

Keith Jarrett got an early start on his path to performing groundbreaking solo piano music. He began piano lessons before his third birthday, and by age five, he had appeared on a TV talent show hosted by the swing bandleader Paul Whiteman. By age seven, he had begun giving formal piano recitals.

In 1966, when everyone was going to see the Beatles in concert, the Beatles were going to see Keith Jarrett doing his thing with the Charles Lloyd Quartet at the Royal Albert Hall.

The daring brilliance of Jarrett's solo concerts began in 1973 with the immense Bremen-Lausanne performances. Before long, his solo piano concerts had become legendary.

In reviewing the ECM recording of Bremen-Lausanne in 2010, Tyran Grillo offered "Whatever instrument he is playing here seems to let go of any inhibitions in his presence and shines steadily like a planet in its higher regions."

It seems that all pianos, when they are being worked by Keith

Jarrett, become capable of translating retrograde-inverted-New Orleans-boogie-woogie, funk-driven bass lines, two certain hands of smoke and lightning sounding as four hands. Surely there can be no greater pianist, no one better at improvisation.

Jarrett's improvisation is immediate, full-fledged,

on-the-spot composition, all the while on the keys eliciting the end product, hammering, ringing bright and peppery upper register, and salty, sensuous lows.

Grillo adds, "It's difficult to imagine, even now, that his command of the keyboard is such that he is playing what he thinks as he is thinking it."

Notes of joy scurry into pools of reflection and expression; inside of the piano: fingers on the strings, and on the piano case drum set, woodpecker and Cupid rolled into one, the spirit of Thor unleashed, thumping and pounding, surfing wild, intricate figures, the fast draw; who is that masked man disguising the melody line in the bass, flipping the bass over into sunny side up, glassy brilliance, shrill trills above unwieldy intervals, flatted seventh heavens, runaway long-train arpeggios that stop on a dime; evenly keyed, shaping tonalities lickety-split en route, dropping 5th's, augmenting 6th's, shifting and sifting through statistically dense, tonal contradictions to the very heart of the root key, like a fish monger, peddling all the way home.

Keith Jarrett with trios, large ensembles, duets, and orchestra is a revelation, but Keith Jarrett, solo, is beyond comparison. A guide on an excursion into the wilderness, he journeys over difficult, electrifying terrain to surprising, exhilarating, fulfilling magical places where it all comes together in emotional and intellectual satisfaction, a sure cure for all 500 shades of the blues.

Surfing Jazz Radio

A rolling, rumbling bolero

on electronic instruments and

fat, fuzzy brass, and

more, deeper brass;

next,

on the snap, a jazz drummer

on a (2+3) 5

and thriving;

next,

very intelligent jazz,

70's Corea-like, which

That sounds good to me;

next,

Tommy Dorsey from

around 1932 skidoo,

Davey Tough

on the traps-and-shoot,

dealing behind the

sax, clarinet, and

trombone, simply

rolling, romping and

jumping with, and

swinging with,

the enthusiasm

of the day,

a better day than

the days when

I'd never find

four jazz stations

on the radio.

Sonata Sortie

Languishing over dessert,

stray thoughts collide with amorous

impulses, he can't take his eyes

off the woman at the next table,

he caught her looking his way,

it took a minute, but he realized

she is looking at him, and again,

and when he looked her way,

she caught him with her eyes,

she smiled, a ritual dance begun anew,

his mouth went dry, and

he can barely believe it,

he senses she wants him,

and he feels like he's tripping,

double meanings intrude everywhere,

she's only twenty-three years old

but she's drawing him in,

her skin is miraculous,

her legs are sleek and smooth,

and as if she is reading his mind,

she crosses her legs and

her skirt hikes up just a bit,

and he tries to look away,

but he's mesmerized,

and cannot look away,

silently cursing the aging process,

he puts it out of his mind,

she and her friend seem worlds apart,

and appear bored with each other,

they were beginning to look like cousins,

he overheard her tell him that she

liked older men. Did she really say it?

She uncrosses her legs and crosses them

the other way, a bit more thigh shows,

his prick threatens to rip through

his jeans, or get sprained in the attempt,

she's smiling his way again,

a near grin. Can she know he is aroused?

Women, the greatest of nature's beings,

he likes them young; he likes them full grown; they always
surprise, often impress,

he likes them slim; he likes them curvy

and round, he likes them athletic, and he likes them bookish, green
eyes tantalize,

blue eyes, and gray and brown eyes too,

blonde hair, brunette, black, and red hair, long hair, short, permed,
straight or curls,

she's engaged in conversation heavily now; her mouth spews in
rapid-fire mode about

relatives, old boyfriends, religion,

politics, dating, world views, and opinions

on everything, he'd like her to shut it,

owing to the content of her talk, which

also pollutes the view, and he wonders how he could help her
accomplish that silence;

what could she put in her mouth to replace

all of those ill-conceived, rapid-fire words,

so we all could enjoy a little bit of silence,

even a minute or two for the sake of novelty,

he's thinking of asking for the privilege of contributing to a fair
swap that he'd gladly

donate eight inches for five minutes of quiet,

which amuses him when suddenly, faintly,

he hears his name being called, and he hears

it again, it's his wife, and she's saying,

"hello, hello, are you there? Hello," he blinks

until he can focus in from the far reaches,

still drunk on the 23-year-old, he says,

"I was listening, I heard every word, I was

just thinking about what you just said,"

and she seems to buy it, or at least does not

to argue about it, he is of the belief that

young women who prefer older men are
especially wise and patently savvy, an older
man is so much more complete and is
superior in every way to a young man, he'd

like to tell this young woman that she is

advanced beyond her years, exceptionally

and sophisticatedly discerning of the

important things, the things in life that really

matter that is of substance and import, he

hears himself saying to those beautiful blues

and beautiful red lips, and part of him,

somewhere, says, "You're full of shit, you

self-serving schmuck," and alas, he knows

it's true, Father Time has worked on him,

giving him his fair share of senescence, the

sun, and wind, the weather at large, and all

of the elements of living have done the rest,

still, there's no shortage of women, knock

on wood, thanks to nature in its splendor and honesty.

In the Zone

Back in my twenties, I enjoyed going into the old Boston Combat Zone. It was 1979, and the Combat Zone had seen better days, but the fact that it was fading, I think, attracted me all the more.

Two or three nights each week that summer, I'd get out of bed around midnight. I'd slide into a pair of corduroys and sneakers, throw on a t-shirt, jump into my '69 Olds Cutlass convertible, and drive downtown to the Zone. I lived in Boston then, in Brighton, so it wasn't a far drive.

Mostly, I'd hang out at Good Time Charlie's on LaGrange Street, rubbing elbows with the pimps and the hookers and drinking. I loved drinking beer and getting soused in those days, and I loved sex.

Good Time Charlie's had hefty, tatty dancers, but the beer was cheaper than the other clubs, like the Naked I Cabaret or the Intermission Lounge. Even better, it wasn't where the tourists or the one-night wonders went. In Good Time Charlie's, the Zone regulars ruled the roost.

By the night's end, I'd pick up a working girl for twenty-five or thirty bucks. Most of the girls had cheap little rooming houses on or around Washington Street. Some had nicer places up on Cambridge Street near Beacon Hill or in Kenmore Square.

Unlike the down-at-the-heels, neglected and desperate girls I saw working around my old neighborhood in Chelsea, many girls who worked the Zone were generously put together and attractive. Most of them were reasonably youthful and managed some enthusiasm for their work.

I never felt they were only going through the motions, like a prison inmate going through the day. Whereas in Chelsea, twenty-five years later, that is precisely the impression that the girls working the "Whore Stroll" typically imparted.

Happily, the mood was much different at the old Combat Zone, and participants expressed joie de vivre. In the old Zone, a measure of cheerfulness and enjoyment often prevailed.

I drank a lot in those days – it was one way of staying off of heroin – but I didn't drink during the day; I worked. I worked hard and made good money, so in the summertime, I always had a ton of cash on me.

The working girls down the Zone used terminology that's largely ineffective today. Yesterday and today, girls would signal their availability by asking, "Looking for a date, honey?" The difference was when I got talking with them, in the old days, they would have a menu or list of services: "' A straight screw is 30, half and half is 35, around the world 40, anal is 50, French is 45, Russian is 40, two girls start at 60'", and so on.

They recited their menu as if they were giving me the 3-egg omelet specials for morning breakfast.

Then there were details, such as how I wanted the eggs, over easy, scrambled? And what kind of toast do I want: wheat, white, or rye? "' Okay, blowjob – no rubber is 45. You want me to catch it, it's 55. Or, with a rubber, I can finish with my hand for 40.'" Cream or sugar? Sweet 'N Low? Orange juice?

Surprisingly, as far as I can discern, the prices are nearly the same today as they were 30 years ago; sometimes they're a bit cheaper today.

Then again, it's always negotiable. They'll charge more if they get a John who they feel can pay more. If they're dope sick, or if it's late, they'll charge less. It's naked free enterprise at its very purest.

My ex-wife was the poster girl for alcoholism, and she liked her pills, too. In practice, she liked it all, and her drug of choice was 'more.' In this respect, generally, we were a lot alike in those days.

At the time, she was in the habit of passing out in bed, usually before we had sex or before we had more sex. Night after night, it was the same routine. Eventually, it drove me out of the house and down to the Combat Zone.

I never cheated on her in any other way, just the emotionless procurement of sex without the complication of having a relationship. Ironically, although I didn't know it then, my ex-wife was the one having a relationship and sex outside of our marriage. She was passing out on me because she'd been drinking, drugging, and balling all day long with her lover boy while I was at work. I suppose it's better that I didn't know it back then.

To me, I wasn't cheating on the wife. My heart and soul were hers; the midnight runs didn't cut into my time with her. She was passed out and unwilling or unable to carry out her marital duties. Or so my self-serving, rationalizing mind reckoned.

We'd been married only a year at this time. It was a marriage she had badly wanted, yet inside the first months of it, she was knocking boots with a guy who worked at a Tuxedo shop. It probably started before that and was likely going on before we were married.

I'd suspected her of it but had no concrete reason to believe she'd taken it that far. Besides, I was working 100 hours every week, and my head was always full of a thousand details on my business.

Many years later, long after I'd been divorced, and long after it mattered, my sister confirmed that my ex-wife had been two-timing with Mr. Tux.

I howled at the moon in those days. I liked the thrill of having sex with women I didn't know or had just met, and working girls filled that role beautifully.

I saw so many women in those days; if I saw a particular girl repeatedly, it was because we were hitting it off sexually.

Finding working girls in bars or clubs was alright, as long as they weren't too drunk. They were a lot less expensive than a wife or a girlfriend and less trouble. It was uncomplicated sex. Sometimes it was empty or passionless sex, but it was better than no sex and a lot better than ball-and-chain sex – sex within an unhappy marriage.

Before I was married, my pals and I liked to drink at the regular nightclubs and pick up women or get picked up. Sometimes, however, it was more time and trouble than I wanted, and it was hardly certain we'd get laid. So, I'd get a copy of the Boston Phoenix to call the classified ads or go down to the Zone.

Down at the Zone, I didn't have to worry about getting laid. It was nothing like mutually fulfilling sex with a lover, but it was usually pretty good.

After I picked up a working girl, the places where we had sex were varied and creative if they didn't have a room of their own. If I was just getting oral, the girl might sit on the bumper of a parked car or simply drop to her knees on the sidewalk.

Some of the more larcenous types might take me into a peep booth and have me sit on the floor in front of me, trying to rifle my pockets for cash or a wallet while doing me.

The more desperate they were to rob you, the lower their price quote was. But the rip-offs were a small minority, and as a newcomer to the Zone, I quickly learned the scams.

But if it was going to be something other than an oral quickie, a room was a must. I can only think of two or three times that I had intercourse with a working girl outside of a room or apartment. There just weren't that many places downtown in the zone where we could safely have intercourse outdoors. It was a sheer city in the zone, with no garden spot or grove for outdoor play.

I'd get home from the Zone at a.m. or 3:30 a.m., get up for work at 6:30 a.m., and work a full day until maybe 9 p.m.

I sold and built swimming pools for a living. I labored like a dog, working 100-hour weeks. I worked on Saturdays and Sundays, finally taking three months off in the winter.

After five years of building above-ground pools, I formed a partnership with a friend, and we built in ground pools. We added two crews to the payroll to continue building the above-ground pools, too. There was good money in those, even after paying for workers, materials, trucking, and excavation costs.

So, I was making even more money. Financially, things were pretty good. I had plenty of cash to spend on chick-hopping at the Combat Zone.

I could easily, if unwisely, spend a hundred or two hundred dollars a night running wild in the Zone. I was 25 that summer, and the volcano of energy I had at my disposal, sexually and otherwise, was mind-blowing.

The best thing about that summer, as with any summer, is the nocturnal adventures. They always made me feel wild and free.

I can remember feeling it when I was 14 and riding a bike over to a girl's house at 11:30 pm for some late-night groping. Her name was Mickey.

She lived in the next village in Waban, maybe a mile-and-a-quarter away. She lived with

her father, who would fall asleep watching the 11:00 news, and Johhny Carson on TV.

My challenge was to climb up a tree that stood in front of the sliding glass doors, behind which Micky's father was watching the television.

So, I first tried to determine whether he was still awake or asleep. Usually, if he wasn't asleep, he was drowsy and about to fall asleep.

I climbed up to the second floor, just a flat roof with a railing, patio and sun deck. From there, I entered the quiet house through an empty room off the patio.

I'd exit the empty room and cross the hall over to Micky's

bedroom. I'd find her in a skimpy, see-through, sexy negligée, awaiting my arrival in the dark.

I'd have to prod her a bit to turn on a light to get a good look at her. She acted shy but finally gave in and granted me a few seconds of light to view her magnificent young body.

We'd have at it, but the truth is that at 14, I just wasn't ready for her in the way she needed and wanted. She'd been seeing a couple of other guys who were fully two years older than I was. So, her expectations may have been ahead of her capacity to communicate them to me. For sure, my inexperience stumbled over her inexperience.

But we passed our beginner's lessons on our way to becoming mature, sexually active, recreational boot-knockers.

Every night that I snuck into her bedroom was electrifying. By the time I pedaled the bicycle home, I could still taste the adrenaline slamming through my system.

I was feeling that wild and free excitement when I snuck out of the house at midnight to meet up with friends at the aqueduct to go pool hopping.

Summertime. Running across soft lawns that were wet with dew in the early morning hours was pure anarchy and joy.

On those pool-hopping nights, our hearts beat fast and hard as we entered the oddly warm water of our latest chosen pool of surreptitious conquest.

Warm summer nights seem to best produce the feelings that add up to wild and free. They're contained in the adrenaline of danger or in the sensory reshuffling that happens in the dark and quiet of a summer night.

It's in the excitement of the illicitness of the Combat Zone at 2 am or the daring and vulnerability of adolescent sex.

It's in the rush of sneaking out of the house at midnight to go pool-hopping or in the adrenaline and high blood pressure of unspoken crime for fun or profit.

Even a slow poke like me came close to setting a few speed records when I was running over lawns in my bare feet on a few of those summer nights, with police sirens getting louder in the distance.

The Fishmonger in Me

I should have been a fish monger,

proudly working a seven-day week,

fish guts and scales on my apron,

the smell of whiskey on my breath.

I should have been a fish monger,

dutifully selling my fish,

shouting out the day's best bargains,

straight from my cart to your dish.

If I'd been a fish monger,

I'd have had a lot of class,

and wouldn't pick my nose,

wouldn't scratch my arse.

Like every true fish monger,

I'd wear my grey wool cap,

and push my cart with dignity,

at the waterfront and around the city.

I'd have been a fearless fishmonger,

cutting off heads and slitting bellies,

to clean my fish and prepare my cuts,

my apron smeared with blood and guts.

If I had been a fishmonger,

I would have had reasonable prices,

for my fine steaks and artful fillets,

so that you'd visit my cart every day.

I should have been a fishmonger,

and on Fridays, I'd buy flowers,

for my beautiful and loving wife,

to celebrate our fairy tale life.

I wouldn't be a spy or a baker,

a car mechanic, or a pizza maker,

I wouldn't be a restaurateur,

or an Army General, to be sure.

I'd be nothing if not a fish monger,

and most would envy me,

selling the finest catches of the sea,

but the finest catch would be me.

My Mom

In my early years, it was my mom's example that influenced and shaped me in every way. My father was an educated man and worked as a professor of Secondary Education at UMass Boston. The problem was he was an alcoholic and unrepentant champion womanizer. He had absolutely no interest or feeling of duty towards me or my siblings as they followed me into the world, one by one.

When I was 4 or 5 years old, as late afternoon arrived, I'd sit at my father's desk with a book or a sheaf of paper, pretending to read or write. I hoped that when he came home, he'd notice me sitting at his desk working, as he often did, and maybe he'd say something to me.

I guess I was trying to show him that I wanted to be like him, moreover, I was trying to connect with him. But from that early age and even younger, right up to my teens, I never had any luck with it. As I grew older, there was a collateral damage being done to my self-esteem, my confidence and my overall sense of wellbeing, as the black hole of a father's neglect deepened.

It was my mom who followed my progress in school from kindergarten forward. It was mom who got me the drums that I played, and the clarinet I played in the school orchestra. Mom attended the concerts at school, the plays I took part in, and took me to the high school football games.

Mom was the one who helped me join the Cub Scouts and the Boy Scouts, Little League, and become an altar boy at St. Mary's Church.

My father taught values clarification at Umass Boston, even developed some of the curriculum, but it was my mom's example in how she lived, and how she treated other people, that imparted clear and coherent values to me.

Mom believed everyone was equal and nobody was better or worse than anyone else. She talked it that way, and she walked it that way. If a neighbor made a racist or anti-Semitic remark, Mom was sure to let him or her know that she didn't subscribe to such thinking or talk.

Mom had a soft spot for the underdog, which, combined with her love of sports, created her fondness for the Old Town team, the Boston Red Sox.

On a bright and sunny autumn afternoon in late September of 1960, my mom closed the living room curtains to cut down on the glare of sunshine so that we could get a watchable picture on our black-and-white TV. She tuned in to the Red Sox game and waited for the camera to show the man playing in left field.

When the ballplayer came into view, she explained to me that the man was Ted Williams, the greatest hitter who ever played and a war hero. She said that after a long and storied baseball career, Williams was playing in his last and final game.

I was curious and asked why this was his final game, and Mom replied that he was retiring. The concept of retiring was somewhat puzzling to the just-turned-six-year-old me, and I wondered about it. I couldn't fathom why Williams, or anyone else, would close the curtains on their career. I didn't understand why anyone would permanently stop doing something that they did very well and had been doing well for a long time. I guess I simply didn't understand yet the concept of growing old and slowing down. To this day, I remember being somewhat puzzled by it back then.

That 1960 look-in on Ted Williams and the Red Sox was my first exposure to baseball. But by 1962, I was listening to most of the Sox games and had started attending a few games each season.

In 1964, when I was ten years old, my mom took me to Fenway Park for a rare night game, my first. Night games were the exception not the rule in that era, and teams played primarily in the daytime.

Even in the World Series, the games were played in the afternoon.

The nighttime game had attracted a big crowd weighing in at about 10,000 by first pitch. Red Sox games in the sixties averaged between 2,000 and 5,000 fans, so this was the biggest Fenway Park crowd for baseball I had ever seen by far.

Making a festive atmosphere even more exciting was the fact

That one of our favorite players, Earl Wilson, was pitching that night for the Sox.

During the pregame workouts, I got it into my head that I wanted Earl Wilson's autograph, and with mom's permission, I bolted from my seat to get it.

I caught him at the third base dugout, where Earl was getting loose and swapping good-natured banter with the visiting players.

I got his attention and asked if he would sign an autograph for me.

He said he would, as he walked over to where I was standing down front. He reached out for my Sharpie and the item I wanted signed.

The problem was, I didn't have either. No Sharpie and no item. I was totally unprepared and really didn't know what I was doing. I actually asked him if he had something to write with, but he didn't, and there were no other autograph seekers in sight. Luckily, he said he'd wait for me there while I went back up to my mom to get the needed materials.

Mom was taken by surprise by my desperate request but started digging and rummaging in her purse for a pen or pencil to properly equip me and send me along on my mission. Tools in hand, I flew back down to the patiently waiting Earl Wilson.

He stuck his big hands out for the goods, I handed him. He looked momentarily perplexed, and then he just cracked-up laughing. Without a word of warning or explanation, I had handed him a piece of torn, brown paper bag, and a woman's eyebrow pencil. The eyebrow pencil was all that mom could find in her purse for writing with, and she found the brown paper bag on the ground under our seats, which she tore into an autograph-sized square sheet.

He was laughing in a good-natured way, as his eyes searched the stands, and then locked onto mom, who was also in knots. They acknowledged one another, sharing a good laugh, and then Mr. Earl Wilson, my favorite player on the Sox, and a hero of mine, wrote his autograph with an eyebrow pencil, onto a piece of a brown paper bag. The autograph, which I had so coveted, was now mine.

Thanks to Wilson's and my mom's patience and good sense of humor, I had my autograph from Earl Wilson, Boston Red Sox pitcher, and a guy who launched the occasional home run.

I'm pretty sure Wilson launched one into the net above the Green Monster that night. I was ten by then, but Dad was still living like he was a single guy without any children. When he wasn't at the college where he worked, he was home drinking or out drinking and womanizing. It left me without a father and mom without a husband.

Dad may have been content to booze it up and live in his own world, but Mom wasn't, and she didn't drink anyway. Dad's inaccessibility didn't get in the way of Mom and me finding interesting and fun things to do. His absence likely provided some of the dynamics that allowed for it.

Mom and I liked a lot of the same music, enjoyed the same sports, and we enjoyed doing things together. It may not seem like a big deal, but when your dad wants no part of you, it counts for a lot.

One thing we liked playing was badminton, and we played it at home in the back yard. We usually had a net set up during the summer months of the early and mid-1960's.

We went to Red Sox and Patriots' games at Fenway Park and to Celtics games at the Boston Garden. We went to museums, and we went to plays and movies. We went to the beach and amusement parks. It wasn't as if we went every week or even every month, necessarily, but it was a steady stream that allowed us to maintain an active and enjoyable relationship and friendship.

When it came to parents, I had to make do with one out of two. But all of the things that we did together, didn't change the fact that dad was mostly absent from our lives. Mom couldn't entirely make up for dad's neglectful approach. Even though mom constantly tried to get him involved in our family, her efforts didn't produce any results.

Some of the most memorable and fun times we had together

were the concerts mom took me to when I was too young to attend on my own. She took me to see the Beach Boys in 1964 when I was 10. A year or so later, we went to see the Loving' Spoonful at the Carousel in Framingham. Incredibly, they had The Who opening up for them. I was one happy jack and was wowed to see Keith Moon kicking his drums over at the end of their set.

I played clarinet in the school orchestra and drums. It was clear that I was developing a real love for music.

Some of the more striking sports events that Mom and I attended included going to see the Boston Patriots play the Airbus-sized Kansas City Chiefs with Ernie Ladd at Fenway Park. We also caught a number of Celtics games at Boston Garden with her brother, my Uncle Bill, back when the Celtics won the NBA Championship 8 straight years.

It was a wonder watching Bill Russell, Don Nelson, Sam and K.C. Jones, Tom 'Satch' Sanders, and the rest win title after title. I'll never forget coach Red Auerbach lighting up his cigar on the sideline once he felt victory was at hand.

Mom was always there for me, both in the things a mother does, and beyond. Maybe mom did so many things with me, because she was trying to fill in the gaps of things she thought that a father should do with a son. But in any event, we had a great friendship and heartfelt camaraderie, that had started in the 1950's.

When I was just 4 or 5 years old, I recall nights when mom let me stay up a bit later while she made popcorn for us served in a large bowl. We sat on the couch, mom put out the lights, and we watched Rawhide on TV as if we were in a movie theatre. We had fun.

I never thought of it back then, I was too young to realize, but Mom was probably anxious wondering when her carousing husband might finally get home. Mom was just reaching her mid-twenties then, and it must have been a very lonely and troubling time. She never uttered a word to me about it, and if she was suffering in some way, it never entered the world that she and I shared.

Mom and I had many of the same heroes; people like President John F. Kennedy, Cardinal Cushing, John Glenn, and Bill Russell were some of them.

My mom always believed that world peace was worth striving for.

She valued and respected people of every stripe. She passed many of her values to me, and in looking back, I realize that one of the things she valued most was me.

Driving Range Gold

When I was eleven or twelve years old, I was surprised to find myself home alone one Saturday afternoon. It unusual for the house to be empty, especially on a weekend when school wasn't in session. Everyone in the family had apparently gone out somewhere, and none of my friends were around. But despite having the house to myself, I was feeling antsy and needed to get out and find something to do.

It was a beautiful day, even warm by New England standards for late October, so I decided to ride my bike to the local driving range to hit some golf balls. I had enough money to buy a bucket of balls, and even though the sun was setting earlier every day, the driving range had lights for nighttime play.

The driving range was in the next town over, but because it was starting to get dark out, I would have to be extra careful riding my bicycle along Concord Street. Much of Concord Street was a curving, dimly lit, rural street with no sidewalks, and yet the cars really hurtled along on it, seemingly undaunted by its treacherous nature.

The driving range was about four miles from my house and some of the terrain along the way allowed me to do one of my favorite things on a bike; gliding down hills. The best place on my ride for gliding was at the end. The final two-thirds of a mile or more was a continuous downhill slope that made for great gliding.

I was always exhilarated by gliding downhill on a bicycle. It never failed to give me a sense of freedom and abandon to be propelled by nothing but gravity and momentum. Without the need to pedal, there was nothing to do but grip the handlebars and lean back while the bicycle went on about its business. With the wind raking my hair, I'd split the atmosphere going like a bat out of hell. Besides, after three miles, it was nice to get a break from the pedaling. So, while the wheels did all the work in cooperation with the paved, sloping descent, I rode along in a state of excited elation.

By the time I reached the downhill portion of Concord Street, it was fairly dark out. The road curved sharply to the right along the last portion of the downhill stretch. It was flanked on the right by woods rising abruptly and steeply just beyond the road's edge. On the left side, just beyond the blacktop, woods gave way to farmland, which sloped down from the road nearly as steeply as the woods on the other side, then flattened out into an expanse of green fields used for grazing livestock. I'd guess that long ago, Concord Street had been cut into the side of a steep, wooded hill.

Gliding down the asphalt where it hugged the woods, it was even darker than the prevailing twilight. Where Concord Street ran along the edge of those woods, the sun set early.

There were very few streetlights, and those provided minimal illumination. Aside from those few streetlights, there wasn't any artificial light around whatsoever.

It was one of the great advantages of growing up in this era. Holliston nights were naturally dark, and my normal nightly view of the sky was extraordinary. It's unfortunate that so many city and suburban kids grow up without that same inspiring and thought-provoking privilege.

Given the road's sharp bend, and the fact that there were only a couple of feet in which to navigate my bicycle, it really was a rather dangerous spot for a bicyclist.

Given the hazards of riding on Concord Street, I remained alert. But as luck would have it, I didn't see a single car on either side of the road over that last segment of the journey.

As I came screaming down the hill on my glide, the road flattened out and straightened, and the driving range came into view ahead on the left.

By the time I had a tee, a bucket of balls, and a club, it was nearing dark, and the nighttime lights were already on. It was dinnertime, and all across New England, people were home eating their Saturday night hot dogs and baked beans. The driving range was nearly empty, and there were only two or three others besides myself. We were evenly spread out along the tees so that everyone had plenty of room.

Like most driving ranges, this one had distance markers; square, wooden signs on the turf, scattered about the range, indicating the distance in yards to each spot. In approximately the center of the range, set at one hundred fifty yards out, was another marker that was much larger than all the others. It stood about fifteen feet high, and was eight or ten feet across. It had a large square painted at the center.

I was thoroughly enjoying launching the golf balls through the cooling twilight air, and hitting a few good shots in the process. Of course, I was limited by the grip I used; I golfed cross-handed.

Even though I was right-handed, I always batted left-handed when I played baseball, and I played hockey as a left-handed shot. But it was a screwy way to swing a golf club. However, I didn't yet appreciate how it limited me. Despite that fact, even though I wasn't very good at it, I truly enjoyed hitting golf balls.

It was almost completely dark out, and I was three-quarters of the way through my bucket of balls when the evening deviated from the typical script and took an unexpected turn. The steady crack of golf balls being hit off tees was upstaged by the surprising and unmistakable sound of glass breaking.

The large, central marker actually had a small target centered within the middle of it. I could see it had a white square centered on it that measured about three feet across. What I hadn't realized was that centered within that three-foot square was a small pane of glass.

The pane of glass was fairly small, about one square foot in size, and the driving range offered a five-dollar prize to any golfer who could strike and break the pane of glass.

At first, I didn't realize what had happened. I hadn't been to that driving range and didn't know that a little prize money was paid out for hitting the target dead center and breaking the glass. In fact, for a split second, I thought I might be in trouble for breaking somebody's window.

The operator of the driving range who'd been watching from his perch at the outdoor counter of the rental hut, saw my confusion and called me over. As I started for the rental hut, he explained that there was a five-dollar prize for breaking the target pane and that I'd won the five bucks.

I was excited but kind of dumbfounded. I hadn't yet wrapped my youthful brain around it entirely. Meanwhile, another golfer – the one who'd been closest to me – seemed to either be claiming that he broke it or else was unsure of which of us did.

I started to wonder if it were possible that the other golfer had been the one who broke it, but the owner of the place was satisfied that I'd struck the prize-winning shot. He quickly ended any suspense in the matter by telling me and the other golfer that I was the winner, which the other man seemed to accept.

I collected my five-dollar bill – an old one but in very good shape right down to Honest Abe's portrait – thanked the man, and finished off the last few balls in my bucket feeling energized and happy.

I was half giddy riding home and could hardly believe my good fortune. Five bucks was a fair amount of money to me back then. Candy bars were a nickel, and I could buy a record album for less than five dollars. But just as I walked into the house, my mood suddenly soured as I began thinking about the prize money.

Nobody was home yet, but I was gripped with the terrible realization that there was a good chance my father would take the money and keep it for himself. That possibility bothered me because I wanted to keep it. I hadn't made any plans to spend it but simply wanted what was mine.

There were times in the past when my father had taken money of mine. It was never a lot except for once when he cleaned out my bank account at the Natick Trust Company. It was a savings account that my grandmother, Grammy Doris, had started for me, and it had grown to about $250.

I was 7 or 8 years old at the time, and dad had decided that he wanted a screened-in back patio that had a roof, and a concrete floor. The money was for the building materials, and he had various neighbors possessing the time, and the necessary expertise lined up to help him build it.

Other than that occasion, whenever Dad had clipped money from me, it was only 5 or 10 bucks. The thing is, he never asked me about it first. He'd just take it from my dresser top or wherever, and that would be the end of it, except that my feelings were getting a bit bruised. Dad would never mention it, thereby leaving me totally out in the cold, just like everything else in my life where it concerned Dad.

I was too young to recognize that maybe dad simply didn't know how to be a father. Or maybe he was just selfish or stingy about his time. All I knew was that I didn't have any connection to my father. He rejected me at every opportunity. The little bits of time we did spend together were mostly at my mother's insistence.

Sadly, the truth about the money is I never would have minded if he had only asked or had at least mentioned it and thereby acknowledged it. I would have felt proud and happy to be able to help out, but it never went down that way. He was taking my money denying me any chance of getting credit for it. As usual, I was excluded from having any kind of connection with this man who was my father. It was frustrating, and it was painful, and sadly, I was becoming accustomed to it.

Somewhere between all of my competing emotions, I was becoming angry and resentful, although I don't think I was aware of it yet.

On the day I came home from the driving range, I wasn't concerned with the larger issue of the relationship between Dad and me but with the smaller issue of wanting to retain the five buck, I'd just won.

I decided to hide my prize money from Dad. Knowing that my

parents might come home any second, I quickly hid the fiver under the cushion of the couch in the den.

Later, when everyone was home, I was in the kitchen telling Mom about my visit to the driving range. I might have been better off keeping the whole thing a secret, but I wanted to share the story of my good fortune. Mom was my friend and confidant, so naturally I told her the tale. Dad overheard my story, came into the room and demanded to see the fiver.

I was scared. I was afraid that he might get really mad that I'd hidden the money. Nonetheless, I told him the story of how I won the money and why I had hidden it away. He asked again if I would show him this five-dollar bill, but it wasn't his usual outburst. There was a different dynamic in play, and I could see that he was bothered by the fact that I had felt the need to hide my prize money.

I went to the couch, reached under the middle cushion and withdrew the fiver. Dad acknowledged it briefly, and went back to whatever he'd been doing without further comment. And that was extent of Dad's involvement.

I felt bad because I think he was hurt, perhaps shamed, by the fact that I'd hidden the bill.

It was an unusual dynamic for us both to experience regret over an incident within our relationship. In fact, it was the first time it had ever happened. Of course, I was getting older and was no longer a little boy. At any rate, we never spoke of it again, and following that incident, Dad never again used any of my money.

Over the final fourteen years of my father's life, I was in recovery, and it was my getting sober that initially earned my father's respect and admiration.

Dad actually became very supportive of me, especially when I was first kicking and making the changes that would ultimately turn my life around. He endorsed my actions and was there for me, emotionally. It was of incalculable importance to me, especially in the early going.

I was a few months into recovering when I received a birthday card from dad and my stepmom, Judy. I'd been cleaning up all the legal problems I had by surrendering to the defaulted misdemeanor cases I'd accumulated, and as a result was in jail on my birthday. Nonetheless, their card found me.

His support for what I was doing was a new and wonderful experience, and was a microcosm of how I was feeling about the entire process of getting sober. I was feeling so many things either for the first time, or as if for the first time, and dad expressing his love and unconditional support was maybe the first and most important one.

You often hear the expression, 'time heals all wounds,' but nothing would have changed without the parties involved changing.

In the process, I was finally able to live my early childhood dream – my aching desire – to have a good relationship with my dad. And in living our new reality, we were able to leave a lot of pain and sadness behind, and simply respect, love and enjoy each other.

Alien Subjugation

When I was a kid, about 9 years old, I became faint one summer morning when I was walking across backyards with friends in the Orchards, where we lived in Holliston. It was a feeling of dizziness and caused a kind of buzzing in my head.

Recovering from the momentary weakness, I wondered if it could be aliens getting into my brain and trying to read my mind or take over my being. But rather than mention what I was thinking, I kept it to myself. After all, I didn't want my friends tin think I was crazy.

Besides, if I were being subjugated by aliens,

the damage was already done, so why say anything? Better to be possessed by aliens than crazy.

In the days of the early 1960's, imaginations

were fired up and alive with so many stories of UFO sightings, and alien abductions being told. The new era of space flight had everyone's eyes turned skyward. Literature, movies, and television were stuffed with stories of alien worlds, UFOs, and alien visitations. The new frontier of space was proving to be a powerful catalyst in every nook and cranny of our society, including my 9-year-old imagination.

I never thought to wear a protective cap made of tin foil to keep those pesky aliens from reading or otherwise reaching my mind, but apparently, some people actually did try it.

In a movie that I watched last Saturday afternoon on television, "Signs," that is exactly what Joaquin Phoenix and two kids did. They made yarmulka-like caps with pointy antennae tops out of tinfoil and donned them to keep the aliens from reading their minds.

I had hoped to see Mel Gibson also wearing

A tinfoil cap, but somehow, that particular photo opportunity was never realized.

In the film, when Mel enters the living room, we see his brother's headgear and the two kids wearing the protective foil headgear, but Gibson, as Graham Hess, never doffs one of the foil beanies.

The idea of an alien watching me or trying to see into my mind, it should have scared me more than it did, but I guess I considered it just a remote possibility. On most days, I didn't take it 100% seriously. Besides, with the U.S. and the U.S.S.R. ready to pitch nuclear missiles at one another, there were far more urgent worries to parse. Either way, it simply wasn't very likely to happen. It was just a kooky concept that got a lot of circulation back in those days.

There were a lot of times when I was a kid that I had wondered about alien visits or contact. Usually, it was on the heels of UFO sightings in the Orchards, or alien stories in the media, which in turn activated my imagination.

My friends and I camped out under the stars a lot during the summer months back then. If I looked at the sky long enough, I'd eventually see lights at play, which seemed at the very least, suspicious. It was especially true on nights when the sky was clear enough to see deep into the atmosphere, and out into space.

There was an incident when I was sleeping out when I saw what appeared to be three spacecraft. They were moving in unison, each with exterior colored lights that were blinking in synchronization.

I couldn't say what they looked like because I couldn't actually see them. I couldn't make out a fuselage or body and had to rely on the exterior lights to keep track of them.

I watched them astounded for a while they maneuvered leisurely as a group. Then abruptly, they changed direction and, moving single file in a straight line, accelerated at a tremendous rate, heading away from Earth and out of my view.

Out in the sticks where I lived, light pollution was minimal, and the air was very clean and clear. On a typical summer night, I could easily see the swath of stars that is the mighty Milky Way. It resembled a vast and busy boulevard packed thick with jewels of bright stars.

All across the sky back then were stars of all colors. More than a few appeared as big as my fist and dazzled brightly. They were familiar neighbors that came and went in orderly cycles of days and months, making for majestic and reassuring nighttime parades and pageants.

But these days, the only places I've been able to see stars with the comparable clarity of those 1960's Holliston views, are on mountains or other places of high elevation.

The skies that people see in today's world are merely a whisper of the skies people saw fifty years ago, before the light pollution of over-building replaced true darkness. People can no longer look up at the sky and see the universe that's above them, at least not with any depth or clarity.

Viewing photos of planets and stars is great, but it doesn't compare with a personal relationship with the universe built through long nights of one-on-one sky-watching.

Lying on a blanket or in a sleeping bag, while watching the clear night sky for a few hours creates a kinship and affinity with our universe that can't

be obtained any other way.

So, until the technology exists that allows us to illuminate our streets and cities at night without ruining our view of the night sky, meaningful naked-eye observation of the heavens will continue to diminish in today's world.

I only hope that with diminishing one-on-one observations of the night sky, and the heavens above it, there isn't a corresponding reduction of those who feel an affinity and connection to the planet as a result of their watching.

In an age seemingly rife with factionalism and rancor, sentiments of affinity, belonging, and empowerment can go a long way. But beyond all that, just seeing the stars and planets at night is a blessing and a privilege. I don't know that a more beautiful and meaningful view is even possible.

He Was

He was the All-American kid,

the alter boy,

the boy scout,

the little leaguer,

the orchestra member,

the A student,

the achiever,

the one likely to succeed,

the one beaten at home,

the one living in terror,

the drug-using adolescent,

the heroin addict,

the comeback kid,

the scholarship student,

the business entrepreneur,

the drug relapse victim,

the father,

the comeback kid,

the one with the broken neck,

the narcotic medicine addict,

the comeback kid,

the computer programmer,

the father again,

and again,

the narcotic-medicine-for-

narcotic-medicine-addiction user,

the grandfather,

the comeback kid,

the old man

who never measured up.

PHILIP W. NATALE, III

Print Day at the Chelsea Library

The fresh warm pages come out of the printer,

into the librarian's hands, and then into my own,

and those pages satisfy me like hot summer

nights satisfy a fourteen-year-old.

Massaged memory helps focus and clarifies, as do the late

afternoon summer shadows falling

across grassy fields.

The slant of my thoughts catches the slant of

of the light, across the slant of my life. Defined,

and captured for the moment, while captured for

all time.

Worries and problems are chased away for

for an afternoon, for a moment, maybe an hour,

by the gift of fresh, warm pages.

From my inner self, out of my fingertips,

through the printer, into the librarian's

hands, and finally, back to me.

The pages come, and with them, like magic,

the thoughts, feelings, and stories that flow in me, which also brings, curiously, a feeling of accomplishment.

273

Dream Jaunt Verbatim

I was dreaming that I was in prison, which, right off the bat, typically qualifies as a nightmare. I had a big swimming pool job coming up, one which paid top dollar. I had called Jim Fornelli four or five days earlier, and left a message on his machine, telling him when, where, and what kind of pool I needed excavated.

I received a telegram back from Fornelli that was delivered to my cell block, but when I tried to read the telegram and call Fornelli, I found that my cell phone and the telegram had been stolen.

I knew who had taken them, a con called Pinkie, and since he wasn't going to return them, I brokered a 'peace' meeting with the prison's inmate leader, a guy who settles disputes among the prisoners, Mr. Biggs.

Mr. Biggs arrived in the gymnasium to preside over a settlement to my complaint. He would either find in my favor or in favor of the thug who stole my stuff.

He stood between Pinkie and me, then lit a tiny marijuana roach. The roach was so small that most people would not have bothered with it. Mr. Biggs had some kind of symbolic test in mind, but whatever it was, it was beyond me.

He handed it first to the accused who took a puff.

Next, Mr. Biggs hit it, and then passed it to me. I took a hit of the almost invisible roach, but as I pulled it out of my mouth, it stuck to my lip. I pulled it off my lip and handed it back to Mr. Biggs.

Biggs took the roach and said, "You did it just like me, so I find in your favor. Pinkie, give him his stuff back." But Pinkie wasn't there; he had slipped away.

Suddenly, the giant video screen in the gymnasium lit up. Rap music started hammering, and Pinkie's image appeared on the screen. "So, Biggs, *this* is how you sided? You sided with him against a brother? Is this how you're going to represent us? No way! It's time for a new leader with new ideas; a new leader who will represent us fairly."

I could see Pinkie reading my telegram. As he flipped it around to look at the front of it, I could see the text. It read, "411. 411. Call me right away."

Pinkie reached out, pushed a button, and the video screen went dark. Suddenly, the gymnasium lights went out, leaving everyone standing in the darkness. A rumble from down the hall seemed to be heading our way. It was almost inaudible at first, but it was getting louder.

As it got closer, the sound became intelligible; it was a group of women chanting, "Kill the men, kill the men, kill the men, and kill the men."

Through the windows in the gymnasium doors, a grumpy, angry group of women could be seen moving in on us. They were dragging a man's broken body. It was Pinkie, and he was dead. They had a statement prepared, which they read.

"To the men in this gymnasium, you have been subjugating and enslaving our sisters for far too long. A day of reckoning is upon us. If you give up quietly, and you serve us as we require, we promise you will be treated fairly. But if you are unwilling or unable to serve us, you will be killed. You will find, however, that if your service is satisfactorily performed, you will be assigned another service and then another. As long as you can pleasure the sisters, you will live. As long as you can fulfill this role, you will continue to live.

"Just to be clear, eventually, you may all die under our occupation of this jail and of this world. Those who cooperate and service unquestioningly will extend their lives indefinitely."

Mr. Biggs was about to blow his top, I could see he was losing it, so I quietly pulled him aside and asked, "Do you see Pinky's corpse over there?"

Biggs replied, "Ain't nothing but what I was going to do, anyway."

I shot him a look, and then he said, "Alright, alright, man."

I asked Mr. Biggs how many of the guys in the gym he knew.

He said he knew all of them. When I asked him how many he could count on in a pinch, he laughed a sarcastic cackle, declaring, "Man, I wouldn't count on none of 'em.'

"You better hope you're wrong, my man," I whispered.

"What's the big deal? I can service these girls all day and night long. Shit."

"Are you serious, Biggs?"

"No. Just in shock," confessed Mr. Biggs.

Meanwhile, the leader of the rampaging women, a snappily dressed prune face with massive biceps and holding a bloody machete, stepped back up to the microphone.

"Attention! Attention. Form a single line. My girls will come by to collect your ID badges. No ID badge, no way you'll live to see suppertime."

After much shoving and confusion, a line was formed, and the ID badges were collected.

The leader of the woman, who identified herself as 'Cookie,' was about to continue her instructions to the prisoners when a voice over a megaphone roared, "Attention inside! This is the National Guard of Massachusetts. You have 2 minutes to come out with your hands up. If you do not comply, we will remove you by force."

"Oh great. You think those clowns are going to worry about collateral damage," I cried out.

"Not even a little bit. Servicing these broads sounds pretty good right about now," said a

dejected Mr. Biggs.

"No shit," I concurred.

Two minutes passed, as silence prevailed. Suddenly, a loud crash was followed by a squeal, as smoke or some kind of gas began to envelope the gymnasium.

"It's fucking tear gas," cried an inmate.

But the inmate was wrong. People started to shake and retch, vomit and convulse, finally falling unconscious. Pandemonium followed.

Smashing through a double door, the remaining inmates and women rioters burst out into the fresh air and daylight.

Surrounded by tanks, machine gun pits, and 250 guardsmen, the inmates, and rioters were herded into a small holding area. They were in no shape to offer resistance.

Mr. Biggs and I were wiping our eyes, still retching, when Jim Fornelli came striding up, grinning.

"I bet you didn't think you'd see me, did you?"

"To tell you the truth, Jim, I hadn't thought of it. But no, I sure didn't."

"Listen, Phil. That pool – you didn't say where the deep end was supposed to be, house side, or fence side." Explained Jim Fornelli.

The next thing I knew, I was sitting up in my bed, trying to gather my thoughts and remember what it was that I'd been dreaming about.

It was still early; I didn't have to get up for another three hours. I might as well go back to sleep, and maybe I can pick up the dream where I left off. If not, maybe I'll remember it later. One thing's for sure: it was a jail dream.

PHILIP W. NATALE, III

Lady Luck Doesn't Give a Fuck

Lady Luck doesn't give a fuck,

she laughs at your tender affections,

she's a haughty bitch who's

been known to snitch,

she cheats on her lovers daily;

Lady Luck doesn't give a fuck,

she watches the net value of your karma,

but she's flighty and finicky

and she'll split from the program,

without previous notice or warning;

Lady Luck doesn't give a fuck,

but she likes all of your attention,

she'll encourage you to hope

for her cooperation and favor,

and desert you in your hour of need;

Lady Luck doesn't give a fuck,

she has a habit of playing her games,

she will offer you the bait

when you badly need a break,

then abandon you to rabid dogs;

Lady Luck doesn't give a fuck,

she's not someone you can count on,

and when she's all stripped down

to the bottom dollar and bottom line,

she's shabby and frumpy, lame and lumpy;

Lady Luck doesn't give a fuck,

she's chintzy, peevish, and proud,

she really sucks you in when

there's a long shot to win,

then crushes the light from your world;

Lady Luck doesn't give a fuck,

she doesn't give a hoot or a holler,

if you count on her help

to jingle the winner's bell,

she'll take your very last dollar.

Laurie In My Soul

In April it'll be fifty years ago that I met Laurie. It's hard to fathom that we were in love fifty years ago.

We were quite young when the 1970s had been rocket-launched from the maelstrom of the sixties. The world was still trying to sort itself out after surviving the clusterfuck of the sixties.

As testimony, the red-hot lava of Vietnam was boiling forth, and the Nixon tricks of Watergate were about to play out. I was deeply in love and having my very first powerful and transformative love experience.

When Laurie and I first met in April of 1972, we instantly lit one another up in a spontaneous combustion of flesh and blood. We could never spend enough time together. We'd hang out day and night, even when she was working at the burger joint in Lynnhaven.

Champs Burgers was where you'd find me at suppertime having a feedbag. Laurie would hook me up with free burgers and fries. She always looked very sexy in her work uniform, and as a matter of fact, she looked good in whatever she wore.

To me, she was the hottest and the finest babe in the world. We couldn't get enough of each other, whether it was in the bedroom or anywhere else. But we surely tried to.

We tried when we were in the bedroom, on the couch, in the car, in the woods, on the beach, on the empty lot in Kings Grant, or under the tree in front of the Hampton Roads Coliseum. We were young, always horny, and a little foolish, but we did have a lot of fun.

We met at my apartment on Fifth Street in Virginia Beach in April 1972. It was a little duplex in between Atlantic and Pacific Avenues, with the yard facing Rudee Inlet.

I was floored by the drop-dead gorgeous blonde with the great laugh and the cool accent. Her green eyes held an intelligence and humor that swallowed me whole and would soon envelope me in a haze of love.

She was just 16, and I was only 17 when we met, but I've never loved anyone as deeply or completely since. I had moved to Virginia Beach for a change five months after kicking heroin addiction back in Newton. It was the sad end result of three years of adolescent substance abuse. But I had gotten past that and was ready for a new way of life.

I had never intended to remain there for more than a few weeks, but that all changed when I was invited to share the apartment at Fifth Street. It was right after moving in there that Laurie's path first crossed my own.

We started seeing a lot of each other and it wasn't long before we were going steady. I don't know exactly when it happened, but at some point along the way, we were in love.

After we'd been going out for about a year and a half, Laurie and her family moved to London in September 1973.

Her father was a Naval Captain, and he was being posted to North Atlantic Surface Operations for NATO. The posting required that he reside in London. As a result, Laurie was doing her senior year of high school in London and wouldn't return to the United States until July 1974.

We had planned that I would fly to London and get a place to live so that we could be together for the ten months that she would be there.

I had saved quite a lot of money from working, and true to our plan, I flew over to London about three weeks after she did. Unbelievably, I was not allowed entry into the UK.

Initially, when getting my passport stamped, I was pulled out of line so they could check me out further. For the next couple of hours, I was asked questions about myself and about my visit.

When I was first going through customs, the immigration officer asked me if a three-week stay was okay. I replied, "Yes," and then I asked the question that got me pulled out of line and denied a routine entry.

I asked, "What are the rules; say, if I were to get a job, can I apply for permission to stay longer, or should I have done that before my trip?"

So, I was pulled out of line and walked a short distance to an immigration office. I was told to wait on a bench outside the office while they proceeded to do whatever it was that they were going to do.

Over the next couple of hours, they alternately had me in their office to ask me questions then had me wait back on the bench just outside their office.

At one point, they took me to my suitcase, where one of them was going through all of my clothes and belongings.

They pulled out my hiking boots and asked me what they were for. I told them the boots were for walking and hiking. Next, they pulled out my cassette player. The play button had somehow been engaged, and the batteries had been worn out. They asked me what it was for. I explained it was for playing the cassette tapes of music that I'd brought with me.

They seemed satisfied with my answers, and then I was back on the bench, waiting to see what was going to happen next. By this time, however, I was not alone. They had a cop standing guard next to me to make sure that while I waited, I didn't get rambunctious and flee their grasp.

After about three hours, the guy came back out of the immigration office and handed me an 8x11 sheet of white paper. It was an official notification titled "Refusal for Leave to Enter the United Kingdom." I was getting bounced.

My surreal experience was now becoming downright bizarre and maddening, with seriously heartbreaking and crushing in close pursuit.

The notification was brief and simply read that they were not satisfied that the prime purpose of my visit was a "holiday," which is the British word for vacation.

The notice was signed by a guy whose last name was 'Tubb,' and that was it. For the time being, the matter was closed. I was screwed, and I was truly pissed off.

An immigration officer was telling me when the next flight to Boston departed and that I had to be on it. It was a Delta Air Lines flight leaving in an hour, at one o'clock.

I asked him if I had any right to appeal their decision, and he said that I did, but not until I was back in the United States. So, I was being sent back to Boston on a bum rap, and there was nothing I could do about it.

They said the next flight to Boston would be boarding soon, but I told them to forget it because there was no way I was going to fly back to Boston on a Delta Air Lines flight.

Five or six weeks earlier, on July 31st, a Delta flight coming into Boston crashed into a seawall, killing everyone aboard. The fog was apparently a major factor, but I'd also heard that there was some question about the ILS.

The ILS, or Instrument Landing System, typically provides

short-range navigation in bad weather or at night to aircraft coming into land.

Although I refused to fly on Delta, they didn't seem to mind, and they booked me on a BOAC flight that departed two hours later, at 3 pm. So, I had to kill another couple of hours, but at least they complied with my request not to fly on Delta.

I still had my policeman escort, and by the time the plane started to board, I had two policemen escorting me. They put me in a jeep and drove me to the runway where the plane was parked.

They had taken my passport from me and said they'd give it to the pilot, who would return it to me once we were flying over international water.

Passengers were lined up on the tarmac all the way from inside the terminal. The line snaked along the tarmac, up the rolling stairway, to the plane's entranceway.

The police stopped their jeep about halfway to the plane, and we got out. They walked me the rest of the way past all the other passengers who were lined up and waiting to board.

They walked on either side of me until we got to the stairway. Climbing the stairs, one cop walked in front of me, and the other cop walked behind me.

We entered the plane, and they explained our business to one of the flight attendants. Once I was seated, the cops restated the passport procedure, did an about-face, and went on their way, leaving me to seethe and fume on top of my aching heart.

As the passengers streamed past me, many were looking me over, having seen me a bit earlier when the police paraded me past them. I was feeling absolutely embarrassed, humiliated, and angry. I was also burnt out beyond tired, as I'd been up since the morning of the day before.

It was killing me to know that Laurie had been in the airport to meet me, only to get stood up by what she thought was a no-show, while in truth, I was being detained nearby by immigration.

They never bothered to send someone to speak to her to verify I had been invited. At the very least, they could have paged her out of common courtesy to let her know what had happened. Instead, she was left to wonder what the fuck was going on.

The whole thing was a nightmare for which the British would later apologize. But the damage had been done.

Although we got back together when Laurie returned ten months later, our relationship never regained the cohesion that had existed before. It was now full of uncertainty, and although I wouldn't know it for another five months, it was the end for us.

For me, it was a terrible end that challenged the quality of my mental health and tested my happiness and reasons for living.

My drinking was partly to blame, as I had descended into heavy drinking as surely as I had fallen into drugs several years earlier.

I had no idea then that the alcohol I shared socially with Laurie and our friends was merely a replacement for the heroin I'd left behind three years earlier.

For me, the alcohol was fraught with even more problems than dope. Given the blackouts, my behavior could be bizarre and criminal. At times, the consequences were compromising and shameful.

Laurie had been talking with my father on the phone, and he'd been telling her that I was an alcoholic and someone to be avoided.

By this point in time, I guess she was looking for reasons to leave me. It wasn't like I wasn't a heavy drinker. The fact is, we did a lot of heavy drinking together.

But to whatever degree my drinking was an issue for Laurie, it was the year we were apart that did us in. She simply seemed to have lost her love for me during the time she was in England.

After visiting her at college in Greenville, NC, every other weekend, it was clear that she had new friends of her own and guys who were interested in her at school. They were around her at least five days a week, while I was managing just two.

To paraphrase what Chaucer said in the Canterbury Tales, 'always the near sly one distracts the devoted from the distant loved one.'

She never verbalized breaking it off with me, but her actions were plenty loud. By March of 1975, I was banished from her heart and thus banished from love and from happiness. I was relegated to coping and learning to live without her.

It would take me a long time before I could shake her out of my system. It was a gradual and mostly unhappy process.

Being in love with Laurie was a lofty experience up in the nether world of deep and desperate love. We truly were, for a time, living in a world of two.

Dizzy Dance

At middle age

the old battles with dad

carry on,

the continuing tension,

stretches across the decades,

like telephone wire strung out,

along the utility pole years,

black headlines that point the way of,

the familiar attacks,

the dramatic phrases –

"you're a disgrace to mankind,"

the jibes strike the son,

eggs between the eyes, messy at worst,

still, other times they reverberate

like an ice pick through his mind,

"you're the scum of the Earth,"

until, finally, he reverts back

to Neanderthal,

and he must either fight

or take flight,

the results are nearly the same either way,

be it the eggs or the ice pick,

the old frustrations are heaped

upon new frustrations, and hurt, and

confusion over this dizzy dance,

when he was a youngster, he

fought more than he deferred,

in middle age, he defers

more than he fights,

he meets attacks with silence,

some with vocal dissent,

others by removing himself

From Dad's battlefield,

and thus, from the battle,

either way, enjoining the battle

or departing the battlefield,

it always felt like defeat until,

at long last, the softly ringing bells of

sane realization chimed in that

all rejection wasn't commentary

on what he did or didn't do,

or did badly,

and every personal relationship that

falls to dust,

or fails to attain the highest level,

was not necessarily

a personal failure.

The Electric Purple Fluorescent Concussion Dream

I was a reluctant arms dealer. I was caught up in selling arms to both sides in a brutal, hateful conflict. I sold rifles and I sold bombs, M-16s, land mines, and RPGs.

I never fully understood the conflict to which I was supplying a relatively small amount of the weaponry. It had the general flavor of the stereotypical Arab versus Jew-hatred and homicide and took place in the Middle East.

I had no personal stake in the outcome of the war and had no feelings for it.

It seems the fighting of wars, including this one in particular, just goes on and on over the centuries. They all have the same consequences: somebody wins, somebody loses. Some people get rich, some people gain power, and a lot of people die.

War puts a huge damper on any reasonable pursuit of happiness and spreads disharmony to everyone in the region. Ultimately, it degrades and diminishes all of us.

In the business of selling arms, I was a very small player. But to my customers, I was an integral and vital resource.

For me, it was work, nothing more, nothing less. It was no

different than changing tires on cars, automated factory work, waiting tables, or making pizzas. The pay was better, however, and I could make my own hours to an extent. But the downside is obvious; you can be arrested and put in jail for a long time. Also, you can be ripped off or killed.

The clients frequently threatened me, and as a result, I lived in a world full of fear and intimidation. Every business communication, whether it was about an order, a payment, or scheduling, always had a threat of some kind attached to it. The threats were more than a nuisance, and I was constantly beleaguered by the stress they caused me. They were the primary cause of my dissatisfaction with the business, but they weren't the only problem.

I had wanted out of the weapons business but was afraid to quit for a good reason. Both sides continually drove home their stated intention to kill me if I ever got out of the business. They also promised to kill me if I sold weapons to the other side, which, of course, I did routinely. And for my sins, I lived a repeating death.

In this dream or nightmare, my death occurred in one of two ways repeatedly. The first was a rifle shot to the head at point-blank range, fired from an M-16 by a woman in a hotel corridor most unexpectedly. In the second scenario, I was trapped with others in the lobby of a hotel. The hotel had just been bombed, and the roof and upper floors were coming down on us.

I only had this nightmare once that I'm aware of. It was in the winter of 1998-99, during a six-month-long concussion episode. I frequently didn't get very much sleep during this period, and when I did, it might be for only 10 – 20 minutes. Often, in that short snatch of sleep, I'd dream.

My brain had been injured from several concussions that I'd had in the early 1990's. Subsequently, between 1994 and 2002, I was in a concussed daze about half the time. This had quite an impact on my sleeping and dreaming, as well as on my mental and emotional health, especially in the long term.

Awakened by the nightmare, I was shaking and nearly terrified. I got dressed and went out to catch my usual bus to Malden Station. When I arrived at the bus stop twenty minutes later, my knees were still quivering, and I thought, noticeably so. But it was wintertime, and everyone at the bus stop was bundled up, as was I, so it's unlikely anyone actually noticed me shaking, literally, in my boots. But I was certainly aware of it.

It took over an hour for the terror to fizzle out of my bones and longer than that before I could begin to relax. I can't recall ever being that frightened by a dream since I was a child, and maybe not even then. It stands out as no other dream or nightmare for seeming so very real and for affecting me to such a degree. It has never reoccurred, and I hope it never does.

The setting, or landscape of the nightmare, was as follows. I am walking down a deserted hotel corridor. It's a long corridor with rooms on either side and a few mirrors. There are some paintings, potted plants, and small trees strategically placed around. Elevators are located every so often, usually at an intersection where one hallway meets with another. It's well-lit, new, and quiet. I see no one as I'm walking.

As I turn the corner, a woman dressed in military garb stops me short in my tracks. She's expressionless as she sights down the barrel of an M-16, which is pointed straight

at me. Probably in her early-30's, she has long, dark hair pulled back off her face, which hangs below her shoulders. She's wearing no hat or helmet, and her hair is neatly pinned in place. She has a light complexion and is slim and trim.

Her uniform is an olive military field uniform, neatly pressed and starched. I can't tell what color her eyes are, but they're all business and reveal nothing. In a classic firing stance, she faces me at an angle, the business end of her rifle in my face, nearly point-blank. I stand dumbfounded and frozen for a moment. She ends that moment by squeezing the trigger, and BAM, I'm walking alone down the empty hotel corridor again.

This ghastly sequence repeats over and over. But eventually, the scene resets, and it shifts to the hotel's lobby instead of an empty corridor.

I'm standing in the hotel lobby next to an elderly, white-haired woman. People come rushing down the stairs in a panic, shouting that we're being bombed. As if on cue, pieces of the ceiling start to crumble and fall. The chandeliers swing wildly, and the entire building starts shaking. The floors above us are collapsing down on one another as light debris and thick dust arrive ahead of the tonnage that's headed our way.

Next to me is one of the windows that enclose three sides of the lobby. The bottom three feet of the windows are hinged, and they open up by a crank handle to the yard outside.

With the ceiling beginning to come down, chunks of wood and plaster rain down as I get the window open enough to escape. I take the old woman's hand, and we start climbing out the window to the safety of the outdoors when the entire building comes crashing down on us. And BAM, suddenly I'm back walking the empty hotel corridor as the dream has reset, and the episodes play out again.

I'm not sure if I remembered anything of the scenarios after each time through, but I remembered it all when I woke up. I don't know what I was feeling during the dream, but when I woke up, I was feeling upset and seriously shaken.

Thirty minutes later, while standing at the bus stop down the street, my knees were still shaking. It must have been an hour later when I finally settled down, but the nightmare was never far from my thoughts throughout the rest of that day.

Never before, and never since, has a dream or nightmare seemed so real and affected me so powerfully for so long. I can't ever remember literally shaking like a leaf over a dream. It was sheer terror.

I believe the reason for having such an unusual and particularly impactful nightmare was that my brain had been injured. I had suffered multiple concussions, and the cumulative upshot was that I was concussed on a long-term basis.

Between April 1994 and May 2002, I just wasn't right. During that time, I had periodic concussion episodes that lasted as long as six months. I was spaced out, and my ability to focus meaningfully was dicey. My sleep was messed up, and my dreaming was screwed up, too.

Part of the problem was my addiction to benzodiazepines. In addition to the daily methadone I was prescribed, the illicit benzos I took each day ensured that I was over-medicated. As a result, during the 90's, I walked head-first, or face-first, into metal street sign posts and iron I-beams all over the city of Boston and beyond.

I sustained a number of concussions beginning in my late teens related to substance abuse. In my teens and twenties, it was mostly from alcohol and fighting, but by my late twenties onward, my substance abuse was in the form of narcotics and benzos.

From my late twenties onward, I was constantly overly medicated. As a result, my head and my brain took a pounding. I walked into walls, and I walked into door frames. I banged my head on kitchen cabinet doors, overhangs, and car door roof-edges. But the seriousness of these blunt force traumas went up a few notches after April 1994.

I was in the old Hyannis bus depot after dropping my three young sons off with their mom after my weekend with them. I was in line waiting to board the bus that would take me back to Boston when I remembered I had left my Boston Bruins cap on the pay phone I'd used in the lobby.

We routinely boarded the busses in the two-bus garage at the old Hyannis bus depot, so I left my place in line to go back to the lobby to retrieve my cap. The line that started at the door of the bus was only four or five people long, and I'd be back in less than two minutes.

I recovered the cap, and from the lobby, I could see that the people lined up at the bus had started boarding. So, I started running back down the long hallway to the bus garage. As I neared the garage, I was stopped in my tracks by an air conditioner sticking out of the wall at head height. I hadn't seen the air conditioner, and I certainly didn't expect that an air conditioner would be venting into the building where people walked. I was running along the wall to avoid the general foot traffic when I ran into it head-first.

I would have fallen down, but by leaning against the wall, I was able to stay upright. After a couple of minutes, I was able to collect myself and continued to the bus.

I had taken one hell of a wallop and already had a vicious headache. I bought an

ice-cold can of coke in the machine to hold to my forehead and boarded the bus for the ride to Boston.

Surprisingly, by the time we reached South Station in Boston, the headache was gone. But when I woke up the next morning, the headache was back, along with a concussion. I didn't know it yet, but I was at the beginning of eight years of on-again, off-again concussions.

Over the next five or six years, if it was solid and immovable, I'd find it with my head or face, sooner or later. It was the result of being truly stupendously buzzed and unaware, or in other words, over-medicated, to put it simply.

I often slept for short periods of time, like twenty minutes. And within that short time asleep, I dreamed. Often back then, my dreams took on a purple fluorescent tinge or sometimes a pink fluorescence. I believe I had some strange dreams in those days, but I don't recall any specifically, except this one dream in particular.

Dreaming during a short twenty minutes of sleep, or even less, contradicted what I thought I knew about REM sleep and dreaming. Supposedly, more than twenty minutes were required to achieve REM and the dream state, but dreaming could happen very quickly for me in those days. s

By the time the end of the millennium approached, I was suffering from concussion-related depression. It was just another event on the skid down to the bottom that I was soon to hit with a silent thud.

The electric purple fluorescent concussion dream was a one-of-a-kind event. It is the only nightmare I've had in my life that affected me so very thoroughly, on an emotional level, for hours after waking up from it.

Almost twenty-five years later, it remains one-of-a-kind, which is a relief.

Giving Up My Right to Choose

The thing to remember about getting into trouble with the law is that you give up all your power, including the right to determine what is going to happen to you. In breaking the law, you give that power to the court and the people working in it. Once you've been arrested, and especially after you've been convicted, the judges, lawyers, clerks, probation officers, corrections officers, and even the trial court officers who work in the legal system all have varying degrees of influence over what happens to you. Some hold more sway than others, but the one constant is that you, as the offender, have forfeited having a say in your own future. It's not always fair, but that is precisely the point; how much respect and fairness can you expect when you have given up the right to determine your own fate?

In 2004, after I'd unplugged from the methadone supertanker and walked off the Benzo's, I set out to clean up my legal problems straight away. It turned out to be relatively painless, but it would take four years to attend to the whole matter, including finishing a one-year probation.

I began cleaning up my legal entanglements on March 1, 2004. It had been one month since I'd quit the methadone program. March 1, 2004, is a day I remember well because it was also the last day that I used Benzos.

I went to the Malden District Court probation department, where I had been on probation. I hadn't been reporting and was so far out of compliance I didn't know what to expect. I could have been locked up and made to finish my probation term in jail. But as it turned out, by reporting, I was considered back in compliance, and told to get myself over to the Cambridge District Court, where I had outstanding charges from 2001 and 2002.

I went to the Cambridge Court and reported to the probation department there. When I appeared before the judge, he set a bail amount that I couldn't meet, and I was detained. I had walked into the court as a free man but wouldn't be walking back out, at least not that day.

Once I was unable to post bail, my path was set; I'd be processed into the jail and given a spot in the new man cell block until either I made bail or my court date arrived.

When I was first admitted to the new man cell, I was given a physical, like all the new fish got, by the Cambridge Jail psychiatrist. My story got his attention, and he could also observe that I was hyper and rough. He spent a fair amount of time with me in a follow-up later in the day

after his initial round of physicals in the morning.

I was in a raggedy frame of mind, and I was motor-mouthing. The doctor, Dr. Spyber, seemed to be a very interesting and learned man. He asked me not to talk and to do breathing exercises. He also asked me to keep my eyes fixed on a spot on his forehead.

Although he displayed a calm demeanor, I think the doctor was somewhat concerned about my condition. He seemed determined to get to the bottom of it.

He questioned me for some time – when he wasn't researching things in a book – and he was complimentary and supportive of my kicking. There was no doubt about it; I was in withdrawal, and I was a wreck.

When he'd finished, I could see what he'd written into his log. He wrote "Post Drug-Addiction Traumatic Stress."

Suddenly, things somewhat clicked into place. The diagnosis made sense to me, and I took some comfort from it.

I was in a confused state of mind, somewhat like tripping my ass off on LSD, with all the usual withdrawal symptoms, including cramps in the arches of my feet that I had to literally grab and straighten out with both of my hands.

My head was ringing on two separate pitches; I was unbelievably

jacked up, and it was difficult to walk and move around. It took every bit of my strength to get up from sitting or lying down.

I had the runs, and my stomach was a real problem, too. It hurt very badly all through the first month off of methadone, and I thought maybe I was bleeding from somewhere in my gut.

I went to an emergency room on two different occasions in the first two weeks off methadone. They both gave me some kind of liquid that magically relieved my gastro distress.

On the second occasion, I went to the emergency room at Brigham and Women's Hospital in Boston, where my primary care physician was. When I arrived at about 2 pm, the ER was quite crowded. I was hallucinating like crazy. I saw yellow, green, and red dots or little circles as if I were looking through a pegboard. The colored dots

were superimposed on everything, and my gut was hurting badly.

While I was waiting to be seen, they notified my primary care physician that I was there. Getting him involved proved to be very beneficial, especially over the long haul, in dealing with my insomnia and post-drug-addiction traumatic stress. But I almost didn't go there that day, because I wasn't sure if I was capable of doing the walking that was required to get there from the train station.

At this juncture, I was almost three weeks off methadone. After taking 160 milligrams every day over the previous twenty-two years, the ensuing withdrawal was very intense.

On my first full day in jail at Cambridge, I was sent to a case manager's office. She presented two or three ways that I could get released from jail, pending my next court appearance, including having a hearing to request bail reduction.

The court system allows for a defendant to claim the mitigating circumstance of drug addiction as the cause of breaking the law. In that event, the defendant goes to drug court and asks for a reduction in bail, giving him a better chance to get released.

I had been warned by others whom I knew at the Cambridge methadone clinic that a bail reduction hearing was a trap that allowed the court to possibly *increase* the bail. Of course, at the time, I should have considered the source of the information. Just as with most institutions, one can never trust the things one hears at a clinic because false rumors and bogus stories abound. So, I was filled with fear and prejudice when I declined the case manager's offer to arrange such a bail reduction hearing for me.

A week later, with the walls of the jailhouse in the new man's cell bearing down on me, I reconsidered that tact. Kicking 23 years of narcotic and Benzo addiction made being locked up even less tolerable. So, I summoned the case manager and requested a bail reduction hearing through drug court.

In less than 24 hours, I'd be heading to drug court for a hearing to see whether my bail might be lowered enough to allow me to be released. It would prove to be a very stressful and nerve-racking affair.

The next morning, after showering and trying to make myself presentable for a court appearance, I was moved to a holding cell outside the Superior Courtroom, where drug court and bail reduction hearings were held.

A different court-appointed lawyer than the one I had for my cases arrived to obtain the facts of my circumstances in order to represent me at the drug court for the bail reduction hearing. The first thing she asked me was, "How did you get here?"

Frankly, I was in a state of confusion. The Cambridge Jail Psychiatrist had one week earlier diagnosed me as having "Post Drug-Addiction Traumatic Stress." On top of that, I was in Benzo and methadone withdrawal. I was truly a mess. My system was sweating out, God knows what, which had an oddly metallic, foul odor. My feet were cramping at the arches, and my heart rate was flying. Breathing exercises helped, especially at night, with anxiety and insomnia. But undeniably, my mind was jumbled.

While the lawyer wanted to know the legal circumstances that led to my incarceration, my hyper brain, which had already been trying to work out the details of a life gone wrong, was working on a much larger scale.

I had been examining all the decisions and actions over a lifetime that led to my current miserable situation, a condition that went far beyond the single situation of being jailed.

Upon being asked how I'd gotten there, my mind just froze up, trying to explain it. Sure, I smoked my first joint at 15 years old, picked up my first syringe at 16, and so on. I was a wreck, and my mind was jammed and jumbled, but I knew enough to know that that type of answer wouldn't do, and I became tongue-tied. After pausing a moment, I answered that I'd been on a methadone clinic in Cambridge from 1988 to 2004 and that they knew me very well and could better answer that question than I could at present.

I was a bit surprised that the lawyer seemed satisfied with my reply,

and I gave her the clinic's main phone number the name of the director, and waited for her to get back to me. There's always plenty of time for waiting in jail.

Putting the attorney in touch with the methadone program had its own red tape and complications. The clinic couldn't speak to my lawyer without first having written permission from me. If they did, they'd be violating my right to privacy and breaking the law. So, the clinic's director read the release form over the phone to the attorney, who wrote it down, gave it to me to sign, and then went off in search of a fax machine to send the signed copy back over to the clinic.

One would think that putting me on the telephone to express my wishes to the methadone clinic verbally would serve to absolve the clinic of any subsequent liability regarding my right to privacy. But a written contract is always preferable to an oral one.

My attorney got the signed release faxed over to the clinic and was able to cut the remaining red tape to get briefed about me and my history.

I'd been moved to the holding cell next to the courtroom along with some other drug court candidates, and they were starting to move us over to the courtroom for our hearings, two at a time.

For the court session, I was handcuffed to a young guy who was there for domestic violence issues. They addressed his case first, and his lawyer made a good plea for his release. I was getting worried that the judge might use up his daily allotment of goodwill, releasing the young man and hammering me back to jail. But the judge didn't like the circumstances of the young fellow's bail plan. He had his girlfriend in court with bail money, the same one he was in the domestic incident with, and the judge noted that fact while denying him bail reduction and release. Trial court Officers uncuffed me from him and took him back to the holding cell.

Next, my name and case number got called, so I stepped up to face the judge. The process was a bit different than the usual courtroom arrangement.

Here, there was a discussion between the court prosecutor and a member of the probation department, and between the two of them, they made a recommendation to the judge, preparatory to each case.

The probation department officers and the assistant district attorneys sat at tables set up in an L-shape in front of the judge's bench as they reviewed each case that came up.

Despite having been muddled and tongue-tied, I could see what was going on, and I found my voice. I represented myself and my situation to the judge, speaking in a measured, brief, and explanatory fashion.

Maybe the judge had seen or heard it all before. I didn't really know. But I explained that I was a lifelong drug user who was breaking from the drugs and the drug behavior that had landed me in that jail. I cited a few short examples from my current situation about kicking, and that was it.

Before my attorney, the prosecutor, and probation people could add anything to my statement, the judge proposed releasing me on personal recognizance. The court had no objections from either the prosecutor or probation, and the judge told me that probation would give me a date for my next appearance on my cases. I thanked him, and my attorney thanked him.

Someone from probation handed me a business card with the date of my next appearance, which was three months hence. A trial court officer handed me a notice of the action just taken, which was bail on personal recognizance, and told me I was free to go.

I didn't need to get any personal belongings because I put on my own clothes instead of jail clothing before the court session.

The attorney told me afterward that she was totally surprised when I spoke up and represented my case to the judge. At the time, I wanted the judge to understand that I'd unplugged from the addictive drugs I'd been on for the past 23 years and all of my life, really. I was making positive changes to a lifestyle responsible for my repeated appearances before the court over the years, and I wanted the judge to know it. For me, it was definitely no longer business as usual.

Taking the elevator down to the ground floor of the courthouse on my way out to the street was a rather odd experience. In the elevator with me were a lot of the same people who worked in the jail or in the courtroom where I had just been. In the crowded elevator were plainclothes and uniformed cops, trial court officers, lawyers, and corrections officers.

After being a prisoner in the jail for the past week, it was a bit strange riding the elevator as a free man with people who had just been guarding me or administering to me as a prisoner in the jail. But as we reached the ground floor, my thoughts turned to the world outside and what I would do next.

I walked over to Lechmere Station on the Green Line, which was across from the courthouse. Before going into the station to catch my train, I stopped at the payphones to call my sister Lauren. I wanted to let her and the family know that I was finally able to make bail and was out of jail.

It was already dark out as I made my way to the inbound train platform. After a messy beginning in Cambridge Court, things had worked out finally, and I was back on track cleaning up my open cases.

After a long day and a long week, I was on my way home. It wasn't exactly a matter of celebration, however, because it meant that I was heading to Long Island Shelter. But, living in a homeless shelter was one of the things I was going to change by getting clean.

In the meantime, it was good to be out of jail, and it was good to be successfully staying off drugs and seeing the withdrawal through to the end. It was the best I could do presently, and it's what I needed to do to get my life back on track. It wouldn't happen overnight, and it wasn't easy. But it was what I needed, and it felt good to be able to look at myself in the mirror and know that I was doing the right thing. It had been a long time since I could say that.

Being locked up and dependent on others for just about everything reminded me of one of the main reasons I had decided to get clean and sober.

I had come to realize that I'd been repeatedly presenting myself to the world, particularly the courts and the police, as 'the nail to be hammered down.' I was sick to death of being hammered down and was lucky that my addiction problems hadn't already resulted in a long jail term or worse.

Indeed, the realization that I had been presenting myself as a nail to be hammered down was an important linkage for me. It meant that I was finally 'getting it.' It meant that I had realized it wasn't that the drug laws were unfair or that the cops and the courts focused unduly on drug users.

While any of that could be true, it was even more true that my arrests and subsequent life-sucking involvement with the cops and the courts were the results of my own behavior. Sustaining a lifestyle of narcotic and benzo addiction is untenable if I wished to stay out of handcuffs, courts, and jail cells. It's a fact of life that I'd finally learned to accept.

Epilogue

I first tried to get sober in early 2004. I knew I needed a major change to straighten out my life, and it made sense to begin by stopping all the drugs that had ruled my existence for so long.

I was 49 years old and had problems with drugs since I was 15. It proved to be a long journey, but by 2004, I was more than ready to change. Every fiber of my being, down to the soles of my feet, was burning-ready to change.

So, I walked off methadone cold turkey after I'd been on it for 22 years. I waited a month, and then I stopped taking the benzos – valium and Klonopin – that I'd taken daily for 23 years.

To fully embrace sobriety, I also stopped taking all the other stuff I took regularly, if not daily, like Xanax bars, fentanyl patches, grass, and alcohol.

The change was difficult, and I suffered through nearly three years of post-drug-addiction traumatic stress, which amounted to a serious case of insomnia and a general state of heavy anxiety.

When coping became troublesome, I got a little extra help by doing deep breathing, which helped to calm me. But there were times when I buttressed myself with a pint of vodka or a dose of black-market methadone.

So, it was close to three years before I got the abstinence part of sobriety right. But I was making progress and learning all along, and eventually, I learned how to live without the occasional drink or drug.

I believed that doing an occasional drink or drug wouldn't cut it because I'd done that a thousand times, and I always ended up re-addicted. I'd been at the substance abuse and addiction game long enough to realize that about the disease and about myself.

It was such an extreme undertaking for me I went to two AA or NA meetings every day over the first six or seven months. In those early months, I really needed to be around other people like myself, people who were trying to get sober and stay sober.

Working on straightening out my life included cleaning up all the legal entanglements that had grown around me. Like a fecund jungle overgrowth, they were always clinging to me, tripping me up and denying me a path forward. It was absolutely essential that I closed them out, no matter the cost.

Any kind of life going forward wasn't possible until those defaults, misdemeanors, and felonies were for once and for all time adjudicated, and any and all repercussions, such as probation and fines, were served and paid. Once all commitments to the court were satisfied, I would be fully detangled from that motherfucking system.

I despised the legal ramifications of drug addiction. It was one of the fundamental motivators in my choosing sobriety. I was bound and determined to never, ever wear handcuffs or manacles again.

I was sworn to never again ride in the back of a police cruiser, get booked at a police station, sit in a courtroom, or face a judge at any time during the remainder of my mortal existence.

I'd had more than enough of putting my present and future into the hands of cops, DAs, judges, probation officers, correction officers, trial court officers, jail psychiatrists, drug courts, and attorneys.

I'd never even been sentenced to a prison term in my lifetime, but the days, weeks, and months I'd spent in jail waiting to get bailed out or released through drug court were more than enough to convince me that the toxic hardship was not to be repeated, or tempted ever again.

I'd always known it, but now I was able to do something about it. I was no longer just an observer or an addicted victim in my own life. Now, I was taking charge and deciding my own fate.

I'd had enough of presenting myself as the nail to be hammered down. I wasn't going to be cannon fodder any longer for the cottage industry of the criminal justice system. They could find their volunteers elsewhere because I had truly had enough.

I had promised myself, when I was first getting sober, to treat myself to a trouble-free, worry-free life devoid of drama throughout my fifties.

I was 49 when I set out to get sober, and I've been able to fulfill that promise to myself.

In the beginning, being free of warrants and unconcerned about police notice was a big deal. Not having to fear my name being run by cops was a new experience. It had been about 15 years since I could last say that.

The fact was, living my life sober reduced the chances of being checked for warrants to practically zero anyway. It represented a large level of worry and fear in everyday life that no longer had to be endured. It made my life much simpler and far less demanding and exhausting.

It was also in those early months of sobriety, when my life was undergoing so much change, that I started putting my thoughts down on paper.

I began writing in earnest about the changes going on in my life. I wrote about the things I was thinking about, and I wrote about the things I observed in my surroundings in Chelsea.

It was helpful to be able to keep track of my changing life by writing about it. It would lead, inevitably, to improved mental and emotional health by allowing me to express complicated thoughts and feelings. But most of all, writing allowed me to keep track of all the not insignificant changes going on in my life. It addressed questions like where am I going, where have I been, where am I now?

After spending two decades heavily medicated, getting clean was like coming out of a deep freeze. In terms of feelings, both emotional and physical, it was as if I were experiencing things for the first time. It had been decades since I last experienced such a broad range of feelings and emotions.

It was miraculous but also daunting to feel things so fully after those emotions had been damped down and muffled for so long. The important thing was not to let it trick me into thinking I needed benzos or alcohol in order to be able to cope with those feelings.

Nearly two years of dealing with post-drug-addiction traumatic stress had truly worn me down. I remember thinking the stress and anxiety that had been hammering away at me didn't seem to have any end at all. It was interminable and damaging. Looking back, it's no big surprise that I had started doing poorly in my attempts to stay sober.

I had moved from Chelsea to New Hampshire in January of 2005. My son had invited me to share a rental home with him in Salem, which I agreed to, but it turned out to be a terrible idea.

It was a neighborhood where people liked to party, and I joined right in with them, drinking beer, sniffing coke, and smoking grass. I was on a dangerous path, especially for an ex-addict.

By the time the winter broke and April had become May, I had gotten very friendly with the couple living next door. By the fall, it had come to my attention that they liked to sniff heroin.

Somewhere along the line, I started sniffing it with them. They were generous, and I never had to shell out any money for the dope. I sniffed heroin

every morning around 9:30, and I'd get another bump or two over the course of the day.

This went on for over three months. I sniffed heroin every day, and it never cost me a cent. But after those three months, they suddenly said that they'd had enough, and they were quitting. That meant, of course, that I was also quitting. And that was the end of it, just like that.

I didn't know if they had truly quit or had simply tired of supplying me on a daily basis. But either way, I had no complaints.

They knew my history, and maybe they were afraid that I'd get in too deep. Or perhaps they really had taken a break from it. Either way, for me, that was the end of it. I wasn't going to bother them for more, and I wasn't going to try to find it somewhere else. The free heroin came to an end, and I totally accepted that ending.

I had never sniffed heroin before. I had always injected it. But I must admit that when I was sniffing it, there was never a time that I considered getting a syringe in order to shoot it.

There were a lot of things that were different about that heroin experience from all of my previous times using heroin. Looking back, it seems the hard battle I'd been fighting for the previous two years had apparently changed my entire attitude and outlook about drugs and drug use.

In the past, when I was using heroin, I never gave it up easily. I'd end an episode of heroin addiction only when I had no choice but to stop. I'd have to be practically carried away kicking. It might be my parents calling the police and having me arrested that ended a run. It might be the court ordering me into a detox hospital that stopped a binge. But simply deciding that stopping was the best course of action, was a course of action I never took, that is, until now.

Admittedly, my prior heroin runs had happened a long time before. Being on a methadone program for the previous 22 years had kept me away from it. But I'd been off methadone for over two years, and I couldn't help thinking that it might be why I found my way back to heroin. My heroin use had been on a very long vacation, but the disease of addiction had never left me.

A week after the end of the New Hampshire sniffing binge, I moved back to my normal surroundings in Chelsea, Massachusetts. The move was unrelated to the heroin binge and was just a matter of changes to the household that I'd been a part of.

But as I resumed my sober life, rooming with a friend who was herself in recovery, I was bothered by my relapse using heroin. After

25 years away from any heroin use, given the opportunity, I had found my way back to it easily enough.

The incident left me concerned about where I might be heading.

I decided to go back onto a methadone program as a defense against any further relapse into heroin.

Ordinarily, I would have been opposed to such a move, but I really couldn't judge things according to my past experiences with methadone.

Unlike in the past, this time, my drug screens would be clean, and I'd be able to earn six take-home bottles so that I'd only have to go in once per week.

After 22 years in a methadone clinic, where I had to go in every day, I'd become burned out with a kind of battle fatigue. Going in every day and never being able to take a day off or go away on vacation was just too restrictive. After 22 years, it had come to feel like punishment or a prison sentence.

However, I was totally confident that my drug screens would be clean because I was going to remain clean. Under those conditions, I would fairly quickly earn my take-home bottles and not be subjected to the daily grind that had burned me out before.

As it played out, I began the program in December of 2006, and by September of 2007, I had earned the right to go in just once a week.

Eventually, sobriety began paying off in a number of ways. First and foremost, I got all my warrants cleaned up and the cases adjudicated. It cost me five weeks in jail at the worst point, as a judge had me detained until the case came up on the court docket. But after a while, I got all the cases closed and finished.

The last time I'd been arrested had been in May of 2002 when I got rousted with a marijuana joint and a dozen Klonopins in my cigarette pack. But since that time, there's never been another occasion where I crossed paths with the law. It's one of the benefits of being sober, and it's a big one. I no longer had to face the prospect of being arrested or jailed.

The longer I stayed sober, the easier it got to cope with sobriety. People started noticing the change in me, and I sometimes got compliments on my improved appearance and demeanor.

By showing my family that I was clean and sober, I was able to improve my relations with them. It started with my dad, who was himself an alcoholic in recovery.

Over the next eleven years, until his passing, my father and I enjoyed the best years our relationship had ever produced. We had a great rapport, and we truly enjoyed our time together when I came up from Florida to visit 3 or 4 times each year.

A few family members seemed to be stuck in the past, and even in the distant past, but in time, they came around. On the whole, my relationships with my family members were greatly improved by my sobriety.

Getting sober had initially gotten me out of the homeless shelter when I became the roommate of a friend in Chelsea. Three years later, when she moved far out of the city, I remained in Chelsea and took a room in a rooming house just down the street.

A few years after that, I moved to a better room in a nicer rooming house in Lynn, which had been my mom's hometown. It seems as I remained sober, I was able to improve my living conditions little by little.

I moved to Florida in May 2010 and got a small apartment in Palm Beach near my brother and sister-in-law's home there. I continued writing with a plan to eventually publish a book.

In March 2015, I published a book based on my experiences with addiction and recovery. I called it "The I of Hurricane Me – Stories & Poems from the Homeless Shelters and Soup Kitchens on the Road to Recovery."

I've continued walking the path of sobriety, and I've never regretted a minute of it. Getting sober was a life-saving effort and the best thing I ever did for myself.

My life was not only improved immeasurably, but I also removed myself from the unhappy and potentially life-ending walk down the plank that my life had become.

About the Author

Philip W. Natale, III was born at the Chelsea Naval Hospital in Chelsea, Massachusetts, to Philip W. Natale, Jr. and Sylvia Lee Natale (Gould) on July 4, 1954. He lives in Massachusetts.

He began composing music when he was 19 and studied music at Boston State College and New England Conservatory, where he earned a scholarship for composition in 1977. His compositions are primarily for symphony orchestra, concert band, jazz, and third-stream solo piano.

In 1980, he received the Boston Police Patrolman's Association Certificate of Merit when he and his STN business partner foiled the mugging/robbery of a woman in Boston.

He ran a swimming pool sales and construction company, but after breaking his neck in an auto accident, he studied computer programming and went to work as a programmer in the early and mid-1980s. After working for the IRS as a taxpayer service specialist, he descended deeper into addiction for ten years until hitting his bottom in 2000.

Mr. Natale first tried getting sober in 2004, at the age of 49, after a lifetime of addiction. After three years of suffering from post-drug-addiction traumatic stress, he got sober in 2006 and now has 17 years of sobriety. He would be the first to tell you that it was a difficult battle.

Natale was homeless from July 2000 until July 2006, when he was able to leave the shelter for good and began reclaiming a life for himself.

He began writing poems and stories in 2004 as a way to keep track of his changing life and his struggle to get sober. This book is about the early years of his recovery when he was first out of the homeless shelter and living in a rooming house full of drug abusers, where his sobriety prevailed. He hopes that sharing his experiences of addiction might encourage someone to take a chance on getting sober.

Philip has three sons and eight grandchildren.